YEARS 5 & 6

FRACTIONS AND DECIMALS

Parents and carers are encouraged to read the explanation and practice sections with their child.

Ann Baker

Illustrated by
Janice Bowles

About this book

Each unit in this book begins with a brief **explanation** of a concept or a strategy. You are encouraged to read this explanation with your child and, where appropriate, to use everyday materials and examples to give meaning to the concepts.

We practise is a worked example for you and your child to discuss together, paying particular attention to the thinking processes required to understand the concept or apply the strategy.

You practise gives your child the opportunity to practise the concept or strategy. It also indicates how well your child understands the new material and often includes problem-solving questions to ensure that your child has mastered the concept or strategy.

If further support is required, you and your child's teacher can devise a plan to ensure that all the basic concepts are fully understood and consolidated.

The **Tests** at the end of the book are provided to check that the concepts are fully understood. Test 1 can be done after units 1–10 are completed and Test 2 when the book is finished.

Meet 'BOB' – Back Of the Book

At the end of each unit, BOB reminds your child to go to the Answers section at the back of the book.

Mathematical Content

This book has been designed to cover the concepts of fractions and decimals that your child will encounter in **Year 5** and **Year 6**. The units provide a comprehensive coverage of the following Key Topics from the **Australian Curriculum: Mathematics.**

Australian Curriculum : Mathematics

YEAR 5

Compare and order common unit fractions and locate and represent them on a number line (ACMNA102)

Investigate strategies to solve problems involving addition and subtraction of fractions with the same denominator (ACMNA103)

Recognise that the number system can be extended beyond hundredths (ACMNA104)

Compare, order and represent decimals (ACMNA105)

YEAR 6

Compare fractions with related denominators and locate and represent them on a number line (ACMNA125)

Solve problems involving addition and subtraction of fractions with the same denominators (ACMNA126)

Find a simple fraction of a quantity where the result is a whole number, with and without digital technologies (ACMNA127)

Add and subtract decimals with and without digital technologies and use estimation and rounding to check reasonableness of answers (ACMNA128)

Multiply decimals by whole numbers and perform divisions that result in terminating decimals, with and without digital technologies (ACMNA129)

Multiply and divide decimals by powers of 10 (ACMNA130)

Make connections between equivalent fractions, decimals and percentages (ACMNA131)

Contents & Checklist

WRITING and TALKING ABOUT FRACTIONS and DECIMALS

Parts of a fraction

$\frac{3}{4}$

The top number is the **numerator**. It tells you how many equal parts there are.

This line is called the **vinculum**.

The bottom number is the **denominator.** It tells you how many equal-sized pieces or parts the whole is divided into.

Fractions are most commonly used to specify parts of a whole or of a quantity. For example:

- $\frac{3}{4} \times 40$ is read as three quarters of 40.
- $0{\cdot}75 \times 40$ means the same as $\frac{3}{4}$ of 40 because $\frac{3}{4}$ and 0·75 are just different ways of writing the same fraction.
- 75% of 40 is another way of specifying $\frac{3}{4}$ of 40.

Equivalent fractions

There are several ways of writing the same fraction. For example, **three tenths** can be written as:

- a **fraction** $\frac{3}{10}$ or $\frac{30}{100}$
- a **decimal** 0·3
- a **percentage** 30% (spoken as thirty percent).

If you have three tenths of $1, then you have 30c, which can also be written as $0·30.

If you have 30% of $1, that too would be 30c.

GAME CARD IDEAS

Cut out the game cards – they will last longer if they are laminated. Here are some games for you to try.

Fraction SNAP!

Shuffle the cards and share equally between two players. Each player takes a turn to put a card down. The first person to recognise and name an equivalent fraction adds all the cards on the pile to their hand.

The winner is the player who wins all the cards.

Go Bust

This game is similar to 21, except that the target is 150%. Each player gets two cards. Each player takes a turn to either choose to sit or to take another card. The process is repeated until both players have said sit or one of them has exceeded 150% and has gone bust. The player closest to 150% wins a point. In the case of a draw, both players score a point. In the case of a bust, the other player scores a point.

LARGEST FRACTION

Place the cards face down on the table. Both players take a card and the player with the largest fraction wins a point. Those two cards are then discarded.

When all the cards are used, the player with the highest score is the winner. In the case of a draw, both players win a point.

Players can use the fraction wall to check which fraction is larger. Change the game and play for smallest fraction, or fraction closest to a half.

Closest to 100%

Place the cards face down on the table. Both players take two cards each and use the fraction wall or the number line to work out their value. The player who has the total closest to 100% wins a point. The cards are then discarded. Play continues until the cards are finished.

The player with the largest score wins the game. Change the total to 50%, or use three cards to make totals closest to 100% or 150%.

NOTE: Games are meant to be fun and provide practice without stress. It is recommended that you stop playing while you are still having fun and then your child will want to play again another time.

COMPARING FRACTIONS

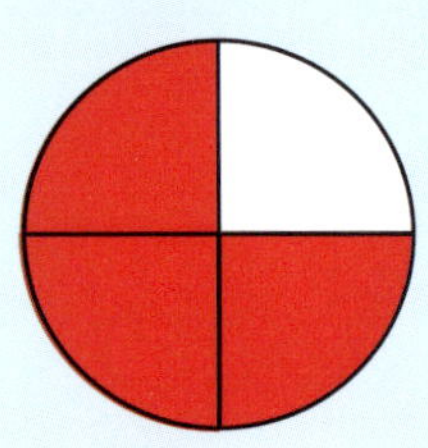

4 pieces in the circle
3 pieces are shaded
$\frac{3}{4}$ is shown

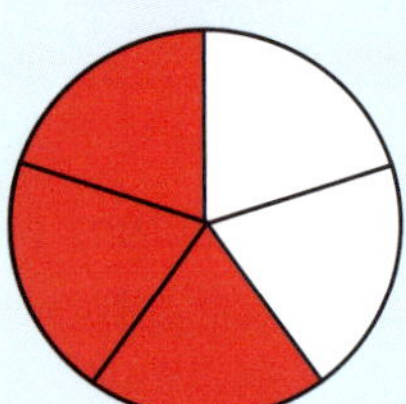

5 pieces in the circle
3 pieces are shaded
$\frac{3}{5}$ is shown

To find out what fraction is shown, start by counting all the pieces in the **whole circle**.

Then count the **shaded pieces**. This will tell you what fraction is being shown.

The shaded pieces also show that $\frac{3}{4}$ is **larger** than $\frac{3}{5}$.

You can also use a **number line** to show which fractions are **smaller** or **larger**.

These number lines show that $\frac{3}{4}$ is **larger** than $\frac{3}{5}$.

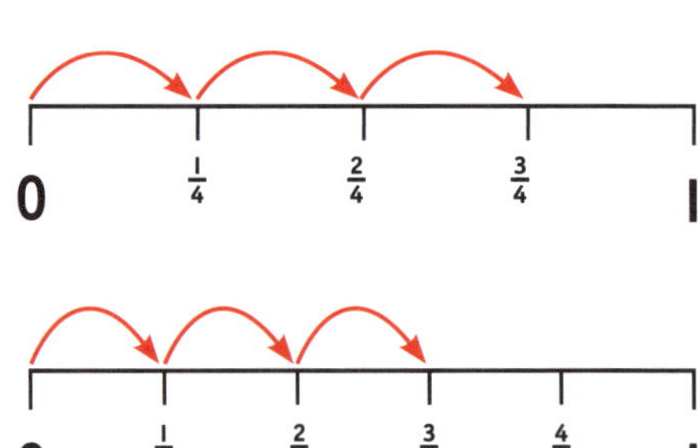

We practise

Shade 7 pieces of this circle.

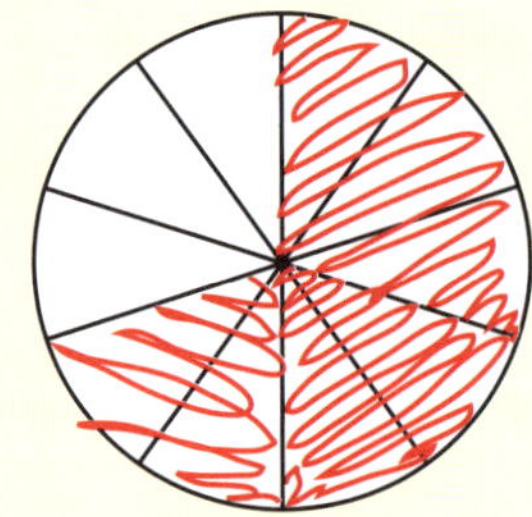

How many pieces in the circle? 10

What fraction is shown? $\frac{7}{10}$

These number lines show quarters and fifths.

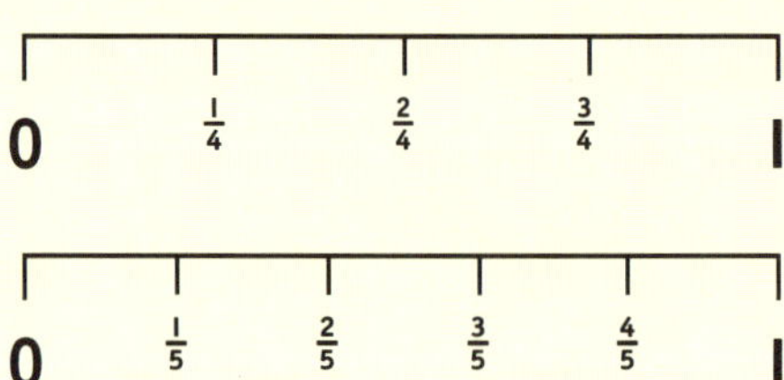

Use these numbers lines to help you mark $\frac{3}{4}$ and $\frac{4}{5}$ on this number line.

Which is larger? $\frac{4}{5}$ Which is smaller? $\frac{3}{4}$

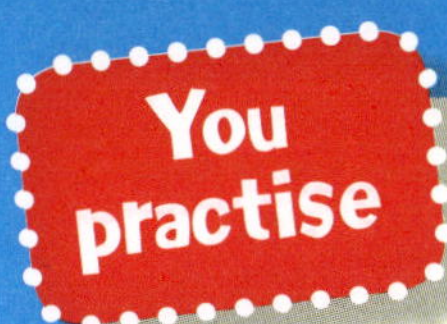

Shade the diagrams to help you answer the questions.

Shade $\frac{1}{8}$ of this circle.

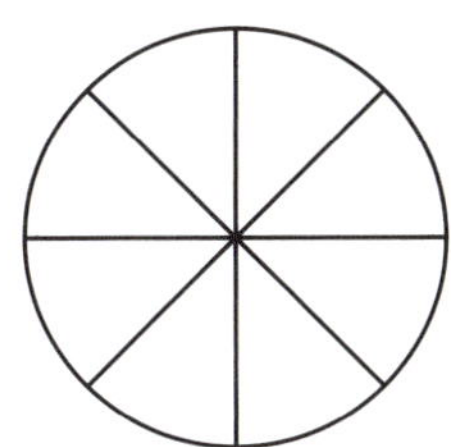

Remember to use the fraction diagrams to help you.

Which is larger: $\frac{1}{4}$ or $\frac{1}{3}$ of a circle?

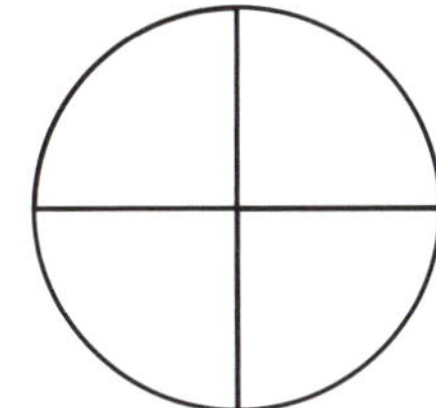
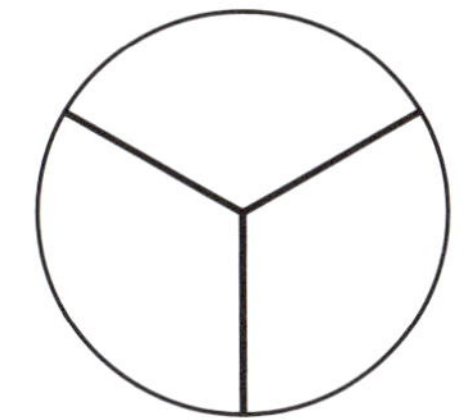

Which is larger: $\frac{5}{8}$ or $\frac{5}{10}$ of a circle?

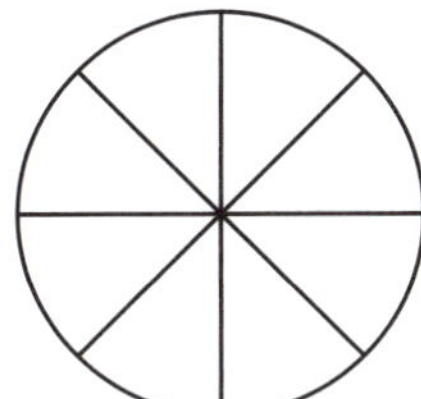
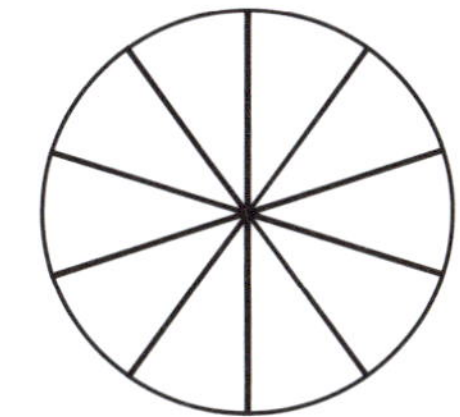

Shade one quarter of this circle.

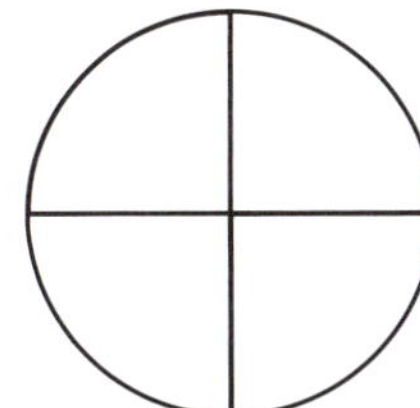

What fraction of the circle is shaded?
How many more tenths are needed to fill half of the circle?

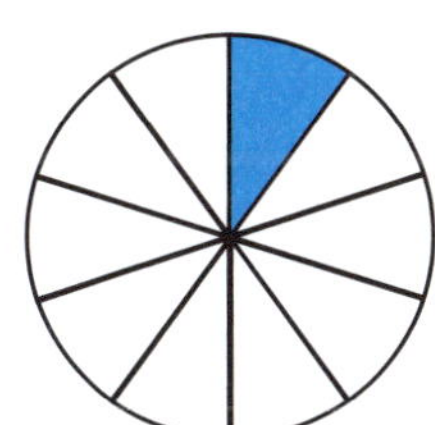

Put these fractions in order on the number line: $\frac{1}{8}$, $\frac{1}{4}$ and $\frac{1}{2}$.

BOB time!

EQUIVALENT FRACTIONS

Half of this rectangle is shaded.

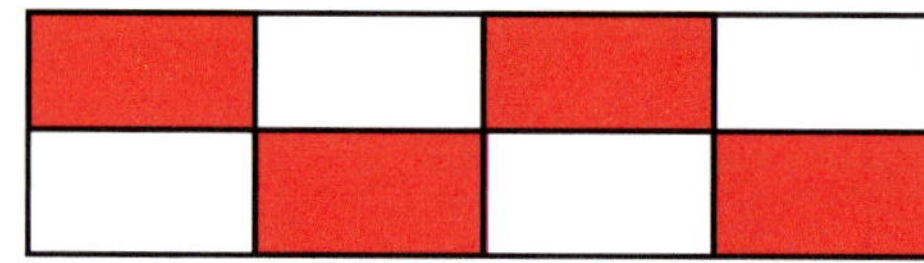

You can prove this is a half by counting all the pieces and then counting how many are shaded.
There are 8 pieces, 4 are shaded and 4 are unshaded. This shows that $\frac{4}{8}$ is **equivalent** to $\frac{1}{2}$.

This one is trickier.

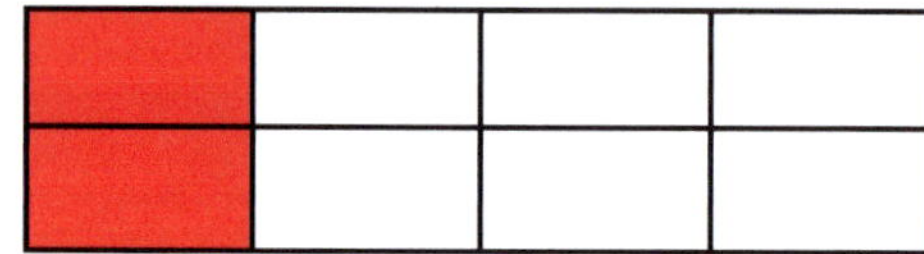

You can see that there are 8 pieces altogether and 2 are shaded. You can see that less than half of the rectangle is shaded; in fact, half of a half is shaded. This means that it would take 4 of the shaded areas to cover the whole rectangle.
This shows that $\frac{2}{8}$ is **equivalent** to $\frac{1}{4}$.

We practise

How many parts in this shape? 10
How many parts are shaded? 5

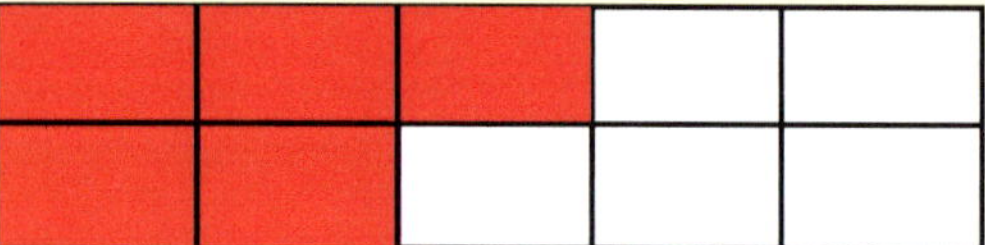

What is $\frac{5}{10}$ equivalent to? $\frac{1}{2}$

How many sixths in this shape are shaded? 2

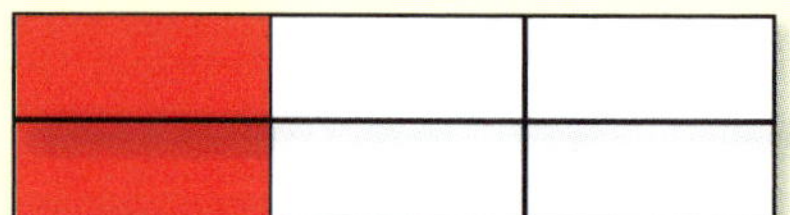

How many shaded areas like this would it take to fill this shape? 3

What is $\frac{1}{3}$ equivalent to? $\frac{2}{6}$

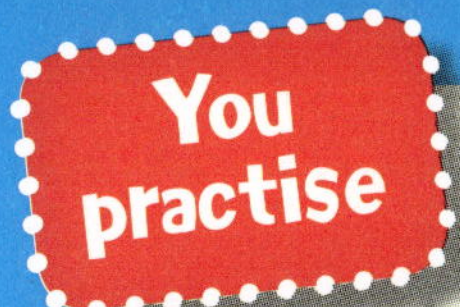

Write the equivalent fractions for the shaded parts of these rectangles.

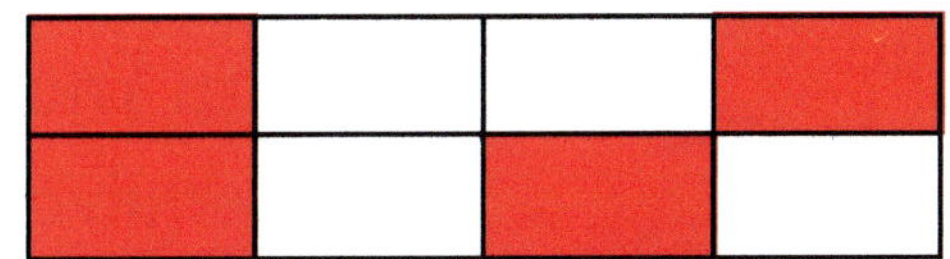

____ is equivalent to ____

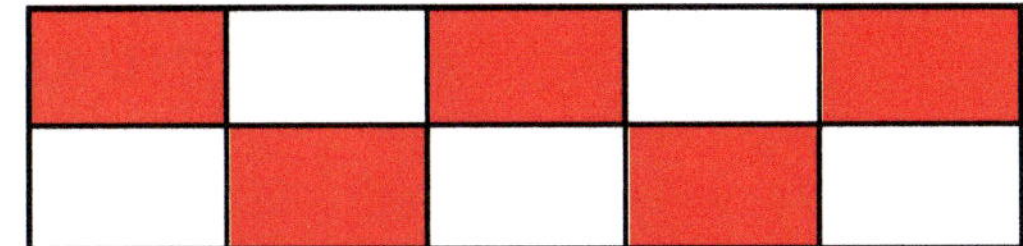

____ is equivalent to ____

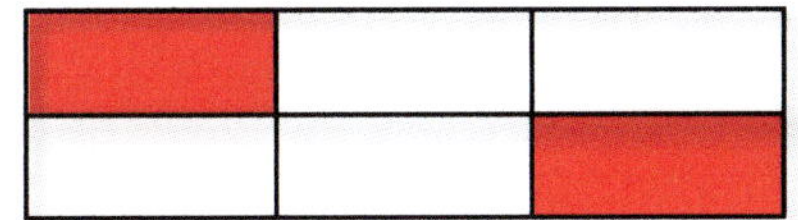

____ is equivalent to ____

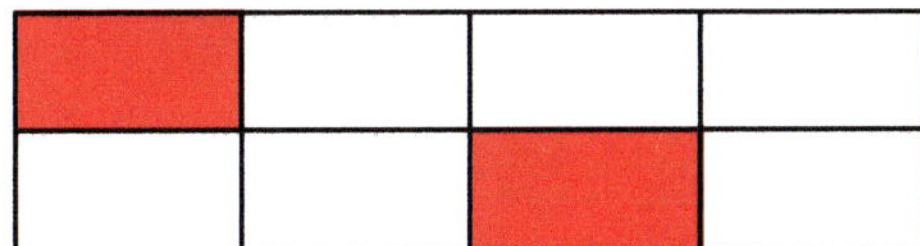

____ is equivalent to ____

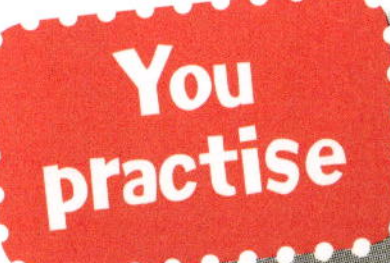

Use these shaded rectangles to show the equivalent fractions.

$\frac{1}{2}$ is equivalent to ____

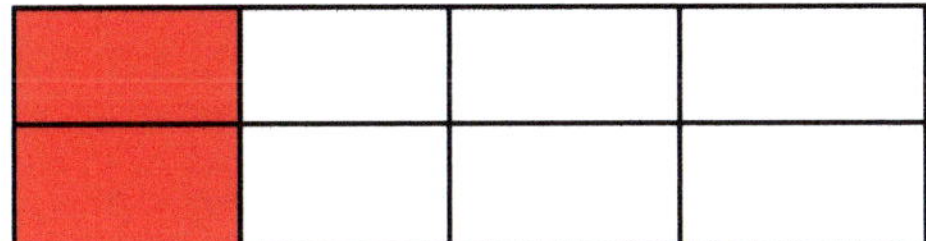

$\frac{1}{4}$ is equivalent to ____

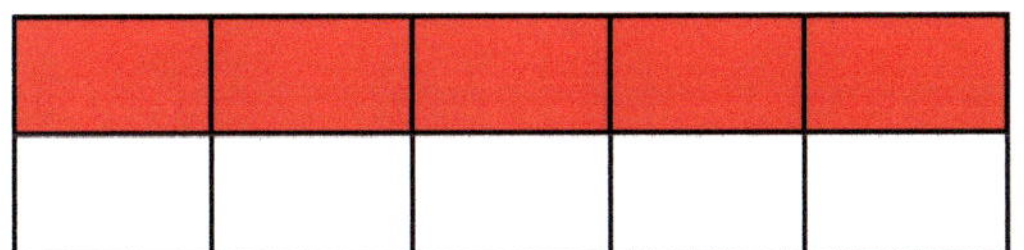

$\frac{1}{2}$ is equivalent to ____

$\frac{1}{2}$ is equivalent to ____

BOB time!

UNIT 3 ADDING FRACTIONS

Making diagrams can help when **adding fractions**. **For example, you can use a fill-up strategy to add fractions**. To work out $\frac{3}{8} + \frac{1}{8}$, first shade $\frac{3}{8}$ of the circle and then shade another $\frac{1}{8}$ to fill up more of the circle.

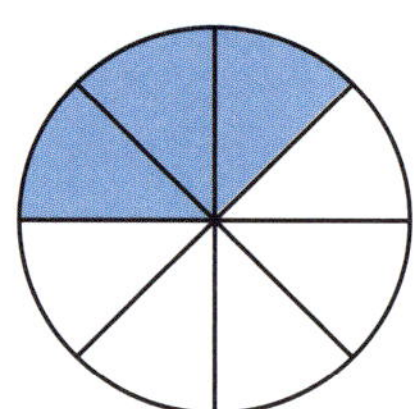

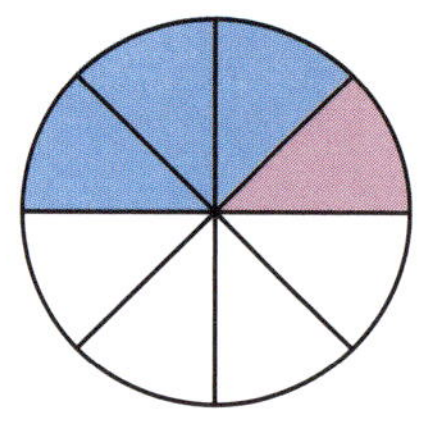

Then count the shaded eighths ($\frac{4}{8}$). You will also notice that **half** of the circle is shaded, so the answer is $\frac{1}{2}$.

This means that there are actually two ways of writing this.

$\frac{3}{8} + \frac{1}{8} = \frac{4}{8}$ or $\frac{3}{8} + \frac{1}{8} = \frac{1}{2}$

A number line can also help when adding fractions.

$\frac{1}{6} + \frac{1}{3} = \frac{3}{6}$ or $\frac{1}{2}$

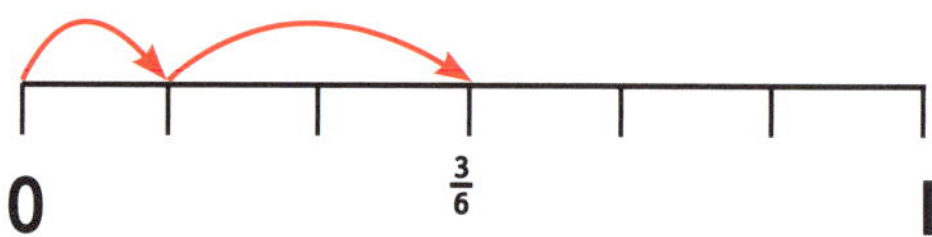

$\frac{1}{3}$ is equivalent to $\frac{2}{6}$, so the jumps are $\frac{1}{6}$ followed by $\frac{2}{6}$. The jumps reach the halfway mark on the number line, so the answer is $\frac{3}{6}$ or $\frac{1}{2}$.

Add $\frac{3}{8} + \frac{5}{8}$ using a fill-up strategy.

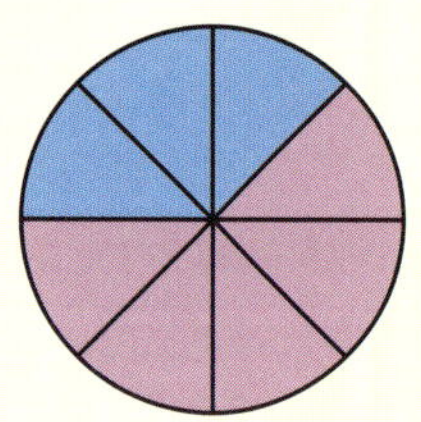

Complete the fraction number sentence.

$\frac{3}{8} + \frac{5}{8} = \frac{8}{8}$ or 1

Add $\frac{1}{4} + \frac{1}{8}$ using a number line.

Remember that $\frac{1}{4}$ is equivalent to $\frac{2}{8}$. This will help you decide where to mark the line.

Complete the fraction number sentence.

$\frac{1}{4} + \frac{1}{8} = \frac{3}{8}$

You practise

Use a fill-up strategy to add these fractions.

1 $\frac{1}{4} + \frac{3}{4} =$ ________________

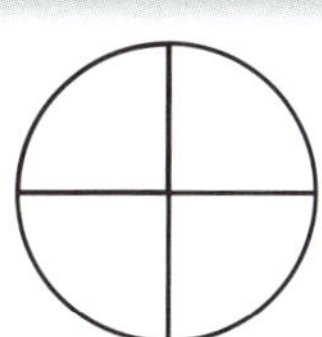

2 $\frac{1}{8} + \frac{5}{8} =$ ________________

3 $\frac{1}{6} + \frac{5}{6} =$ ________________

4 $\frac{1}{2} + \frac{1}{8} =$ ________________

5 $\frac{1}{2} + \frac{1}{6} =$ ________________

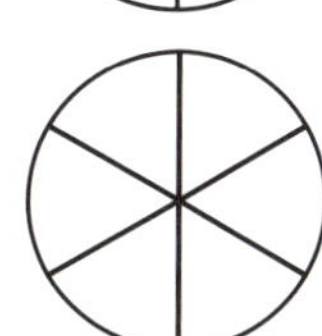

You practise

Use a number line to add these fractions.

6 $\frac{1}{2} + \frac{1}{4} =$ ________________

7 $\frac{1}{4} + \frac{3}{4} =$ ________________

8 $\frac{1}{8} + \frac{6}{8} =$ ________________

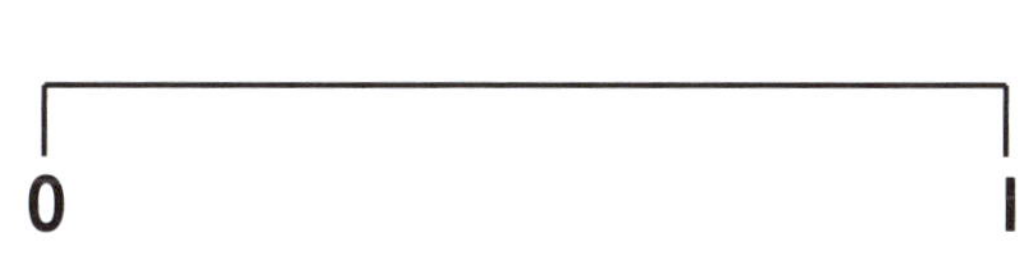

9 $\frac{1}{4} + \frac{1}{8} =$ ________________

10 $\frac{1}{2} + \frac{1}{6} =$ ________________

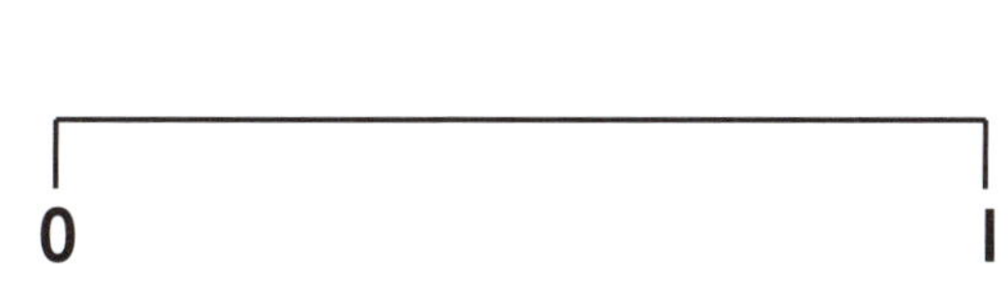

Don't forget to draw in the fraction marks on the line.

BOB time!

LINKING FRACTIONS and DECIMALS

All these diagrams are shaded to show $\frac{1}{2}$. Even though they are labelled differently, the shaded parts are equivalent to each other.

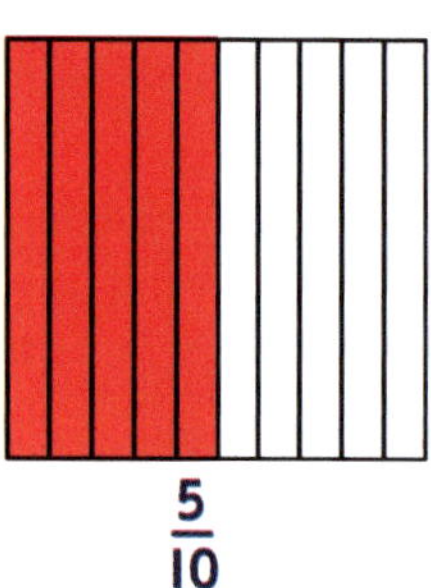

$\frac{5}{10}$

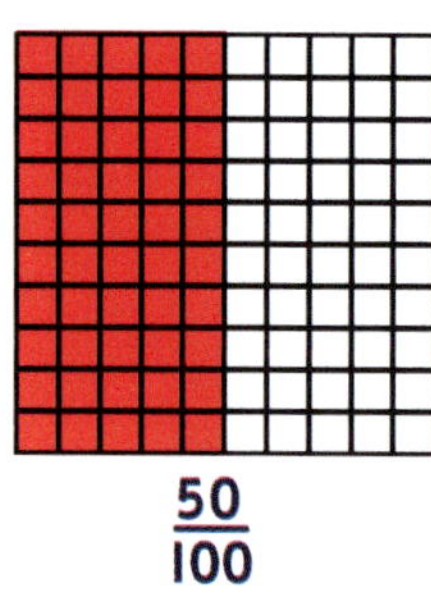

$\frac{50}{100}$

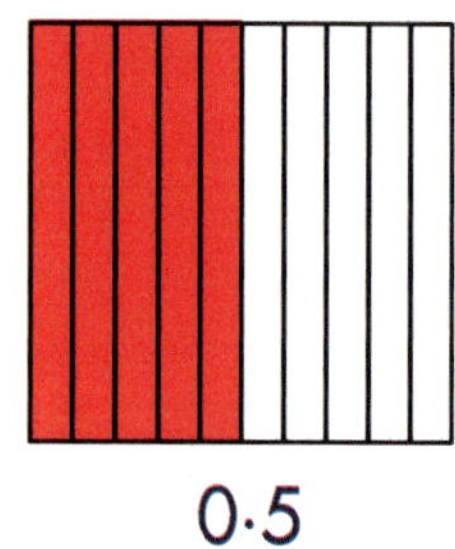

0·5

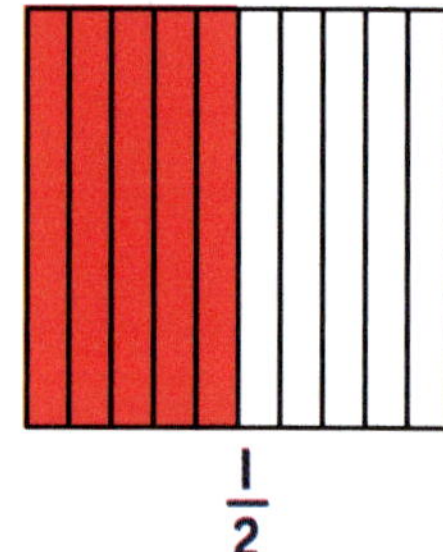

$\frac{1}{2}$

A shaded shape can be labelled as a **decimal**, 0·5, or as a **fraction**, $\frac{5}{10}$, $\frac{1}{2}$ and $\frac{50}{100}$.

The same fraction of each diagram has been shaded, which shows that 0·5, $\frac{5}{10}$, $\frac{1}{2}$ and $\frac{50}{100}$ are all **equivalent** to each other.

Look at these diagrams. They are divided into hundredths.
The first one is completely shaded so it is 1 or $\frac{10}{10}$ or $\frac{100}{100}$.
The second diagram only has 40 parts shaded so it has $\frac{40}{100}$ or $\frac{4}{10}$ shaded.

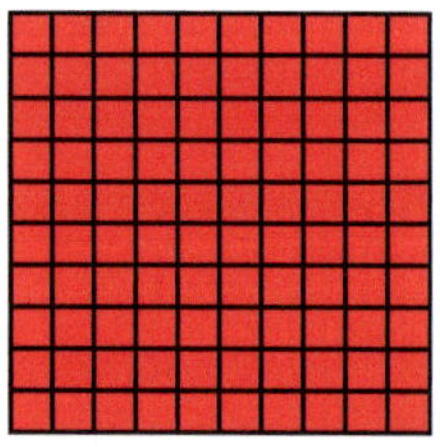

So these diagrams can be labelled as $1\frac{4}{10}$, $\frac{140}{100}$, $\frac{14}{10}$ or as 1·4. These are all **equivalent fractions**.

We practise

Label the diagram in tenths, hundredths and as a decimal.

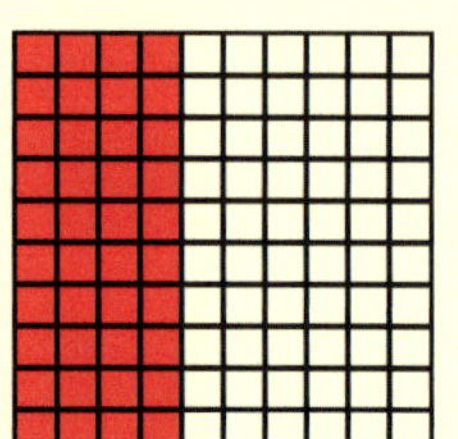

$\frac{4}{10}$

$\frac{40}{100}$

0·4

Shade $\frac{7}{10}$ of this diagram. Write the fraction in hundredths and as a decimal.

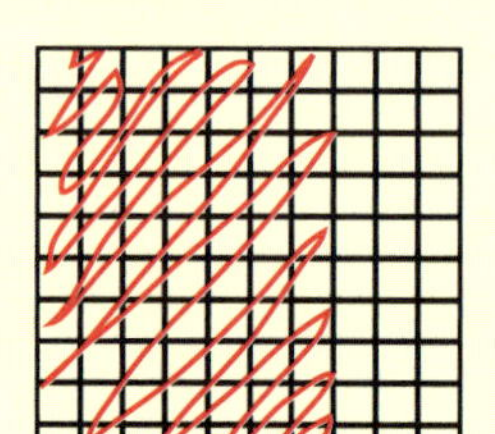

$\frac{70}{100}$

0·7

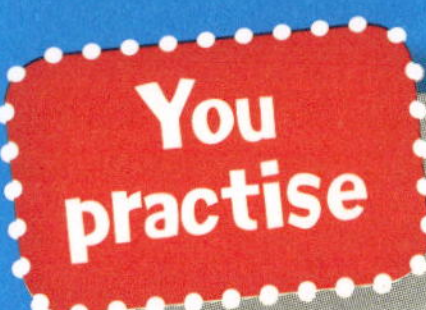

Label each diagram in tenths, hundredths and as a decimal.

		Tenths	Hundredths	Decimal
 1	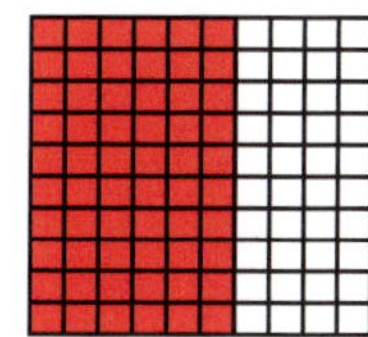	______	______	______
 2	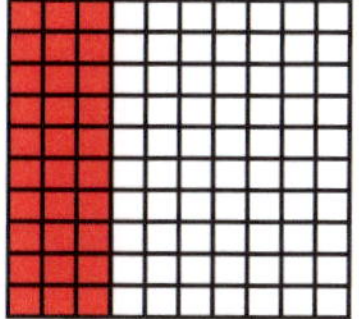	______	______	______
 3	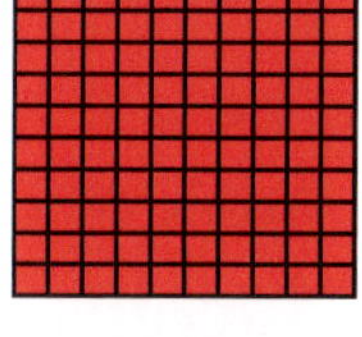  	______	______	______
 4	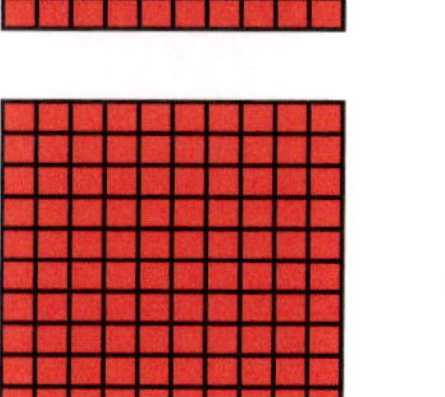 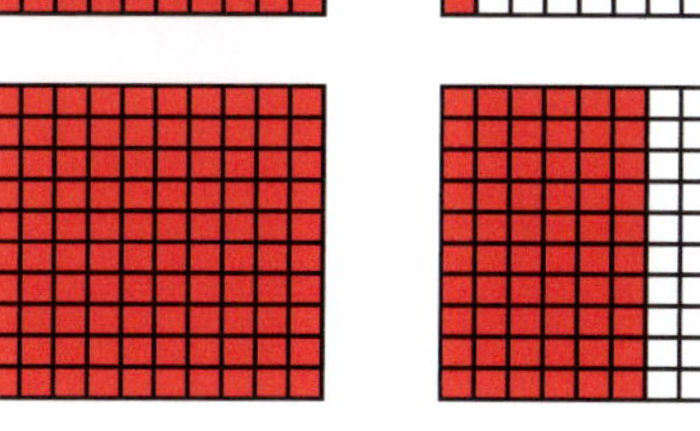  	______	______	______

Shade each diagram to match the fraction and write the fraction in hundredths and as a decimal.

			Hundredths	Decimal
 5	$\frac{1}{2}$	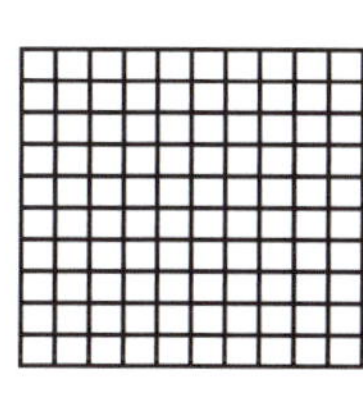	______	______
 6	$\frac{10}{10}$	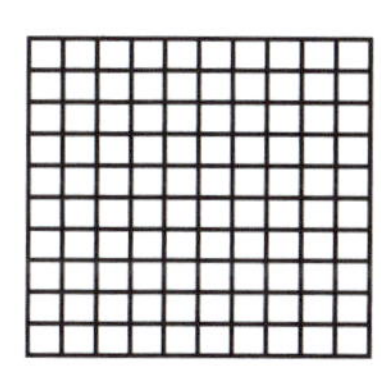	______	______
7	$\frac{12}{10}$	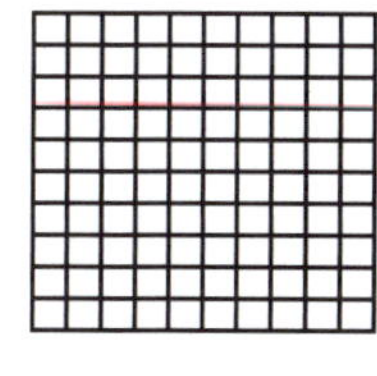 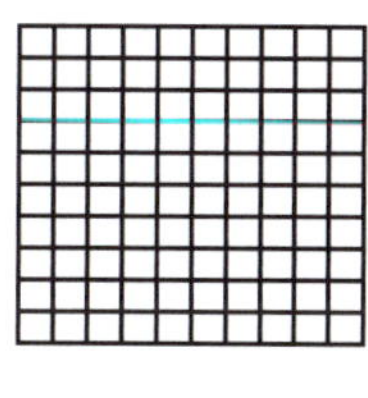	______	______
 8	$1\frac{1}{2}$		______	______

BOB time!

UNIT 5

COMPARING and ORDERING DECIMALS

Diagrams and number lines are useful to compare and order decimals.

For example, you can use a diagram to show which is larger, 0·46 or 0·6.

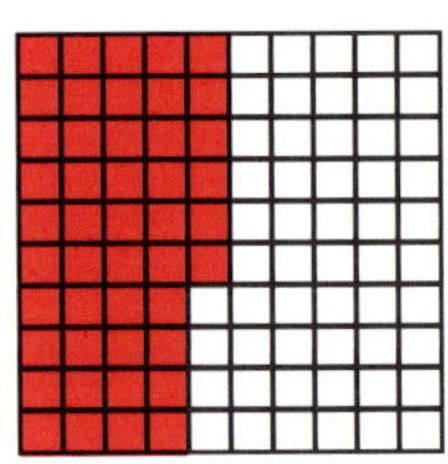

$\frac{46}{100}$ or 0·46

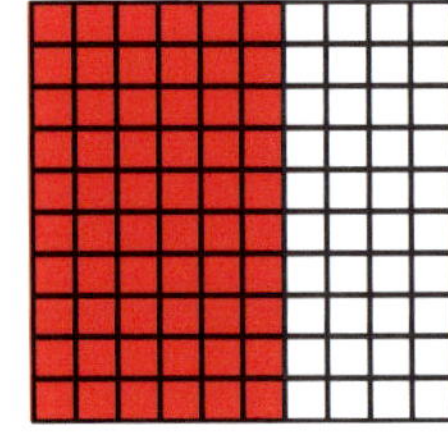

$\frac{6}{10}$ or $\frac{60}{100}$ or 0·6

The diagrams show that 0·46 is smaller than 0·6.

It can be easy to make a mistake when reading decimals. If you read 0·46 as zero point forty-six, it sounds larger than 0·6, even though it is not. It helps to think of 0·46 as 4 tenths ($\frac{4}{10}$) and 6 hundredths ($\frac{6}{100}$).

The number line below has been marked in tenths and shows the halfway point. It also shows that 0·46 (or $\frac{46}{100}$) is **less** than $\frac{1}{2}$ and that 0·6 ($\frac{6}{10}$ or $\frac{60}{100}$) is **larger** than $\frac{1}{2}$.

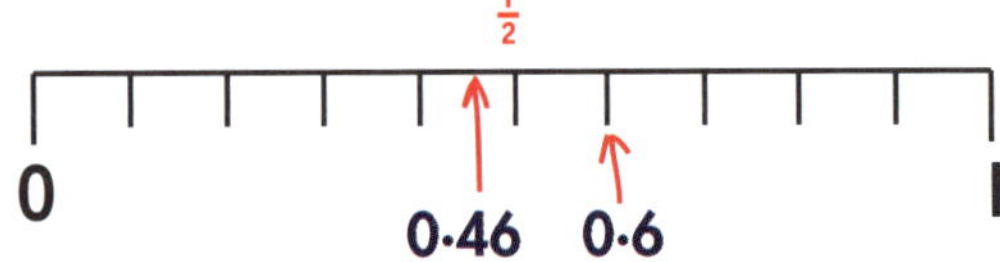

We practise

Use a fill-up strategy to compare 0·27 and 0·4. Which is larger?

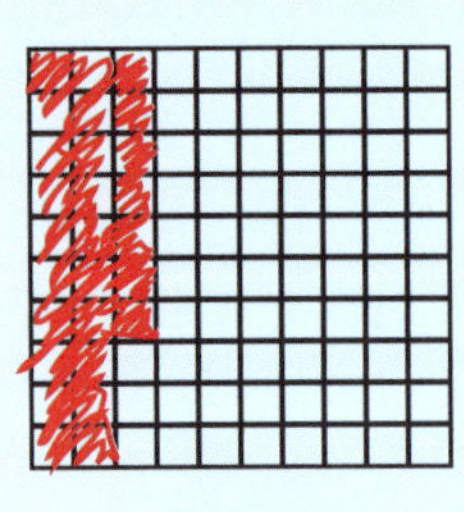

0·27 0·4

0·4 is larger than 0·27

Use the number line to compare and order these decimals:

0·35 0·7 0·85

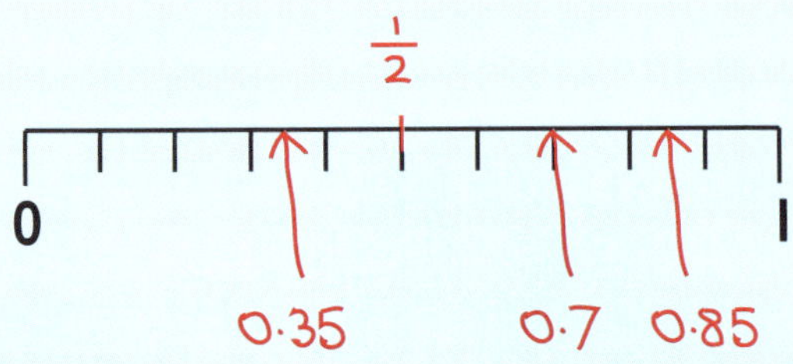

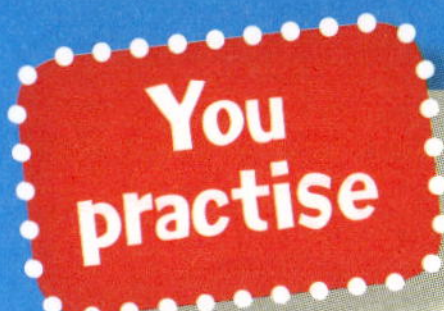

Use shading to compare each pair of decimals. Which is larger?

0·7 and 0·35

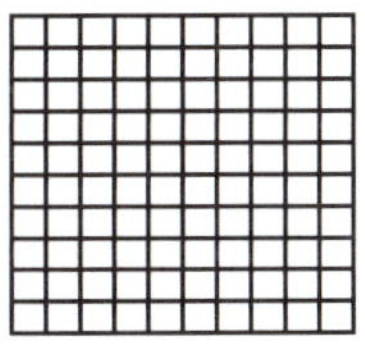
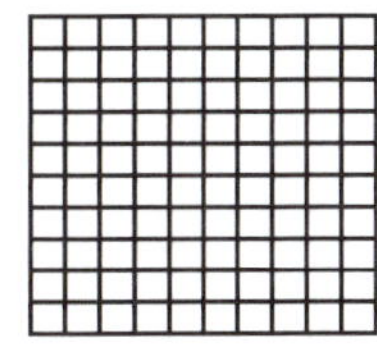

____ is larger than ____

0·45 and 0·75

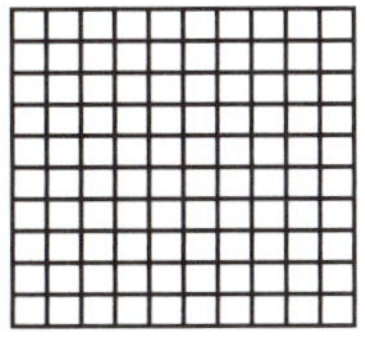
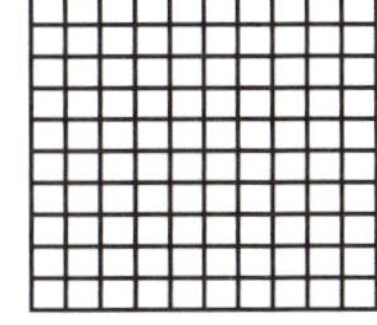

____ is larger than ____

0·3 and 0·03

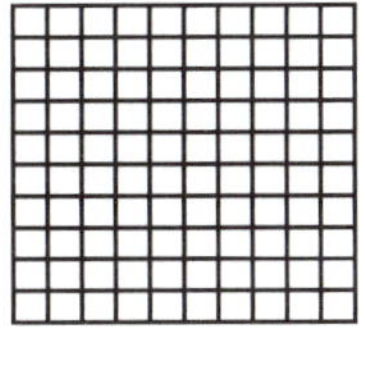
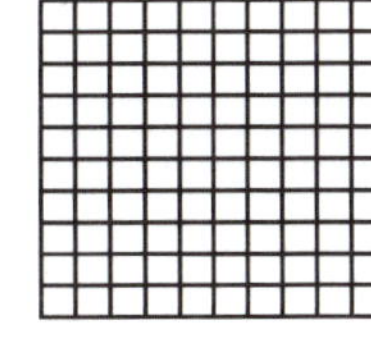

____ is larger than ____

0·8 and 0·08

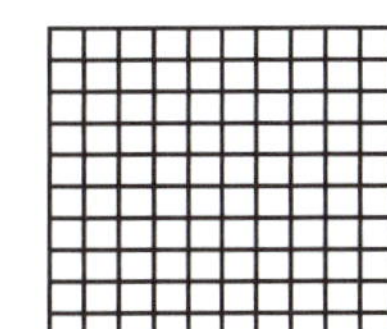

____ is larger than ____

Use the number line to compare and order each set of decimals.

0·7, 0·37, 0·73

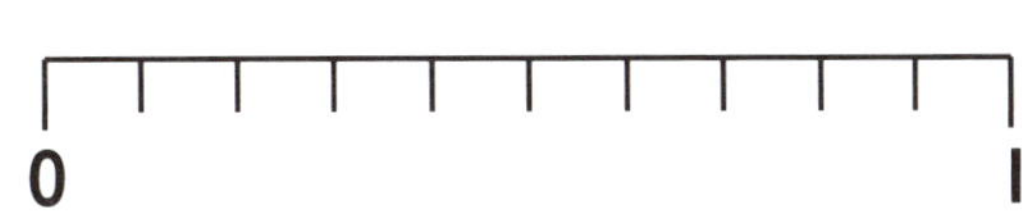

0·55, 0·6, 0·36

0·8, 0·75, 0·89

Remember, it helps to mark the $\frac{1}{2}$ on the number line. So does thinking of the decimal part as a fraction.

0·4, 0·45, 0·54

BOB time!

UNIT 6 MORE EQUIVALENT FRACTIONS

It is easy to find **equivalent fractions** when the **denominators are related**.

2, 4, 8 and 16 are related numbers.

The diagrams below show equivalent ways of shading $\frac{1}{2}$ with fractions that have these related numbers as denominators.

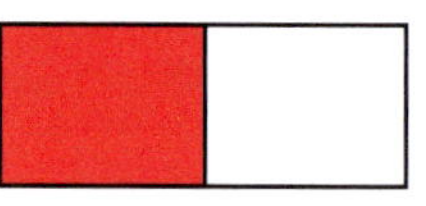

$\frac{1}{2}$

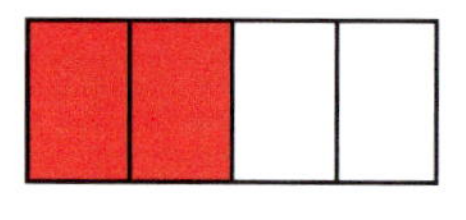

$\frac{2}{4}$

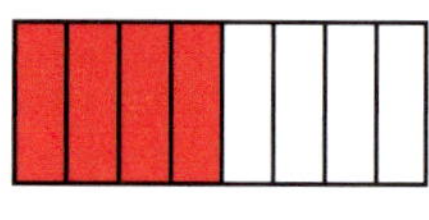

$\frac{4}{8}$

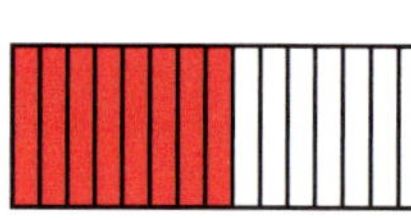

$\frac{8}{16}$

$\frac{1}{5}$, $\frac{2}{10}$ and $\frac{3}{15}$ are also related.

Look at these diagrams to see different ways of showing fractions that are equivalent to $\frac{1}{5}$.

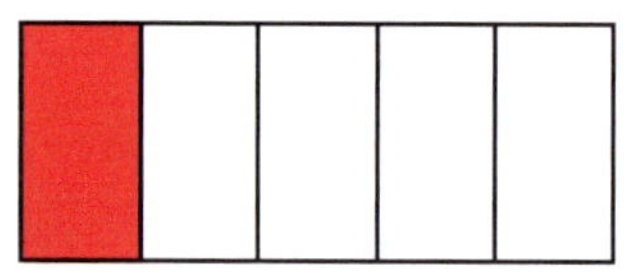

$\frac{1}{5}$

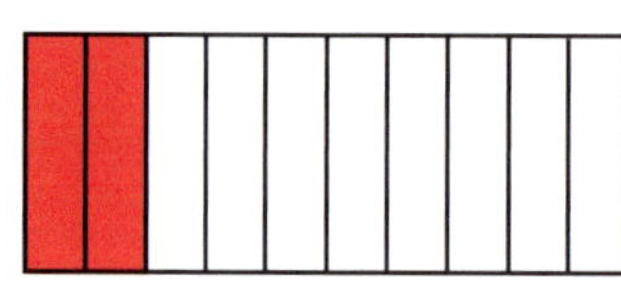

$\frac{2}{10}$

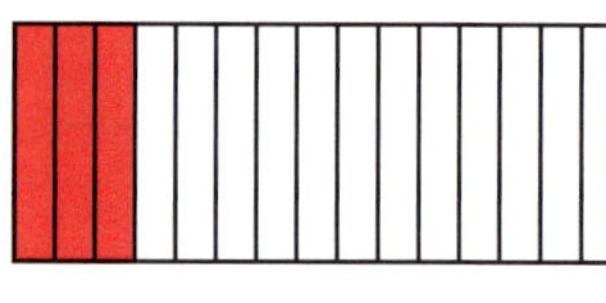

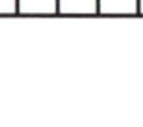

$\frac{3}{15}$

Shade the diagrams to show fractions that are equivalent to $\frac{2}{3}$.

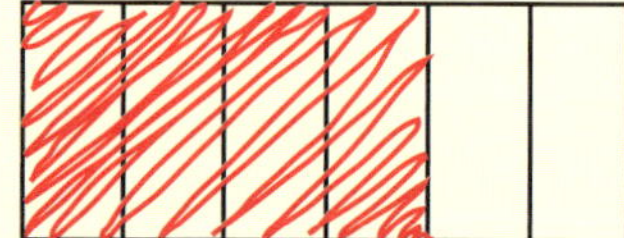

We practise

Shade and label the diagrams to show fractions that are equivalent to $\frac{3}{4}$.

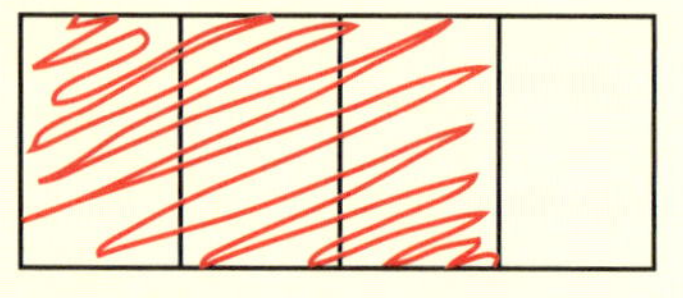

$\frac{3}{4}$

$\frac{6}{8}$

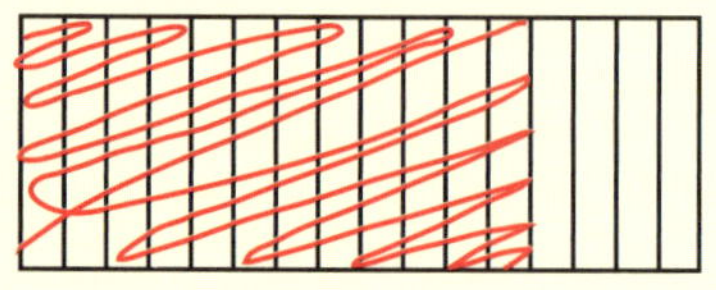

$\frac{12}{16}$

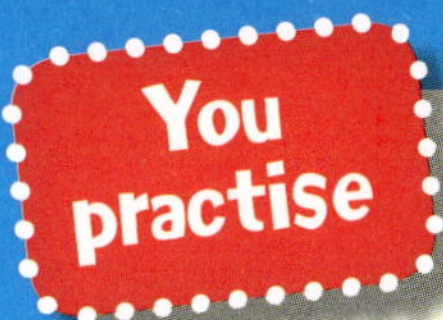

Shade the diagrams to show equivalent fractions.

$\frac{1}{2}$

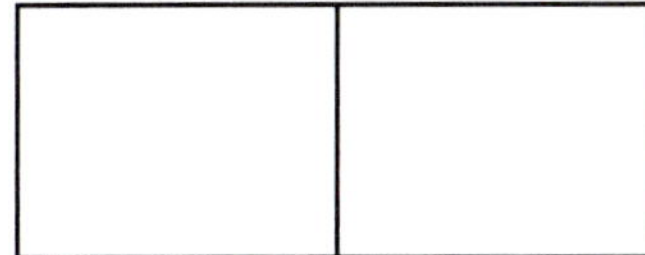

$\frac{1}{4}$

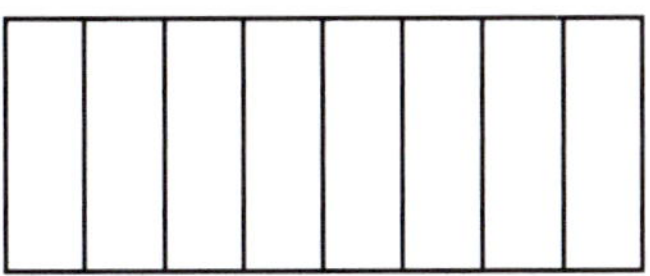

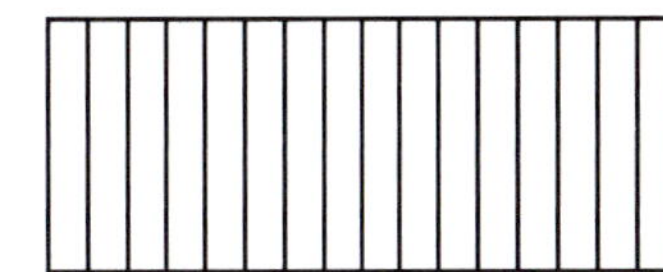

$\frac{2}{5}$

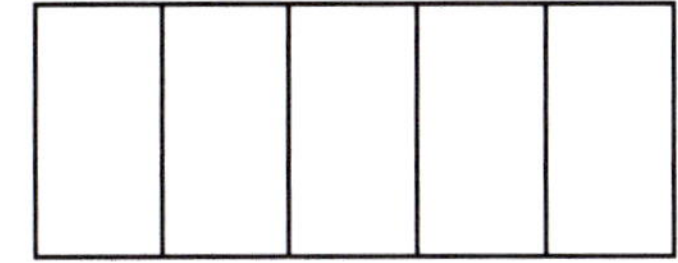

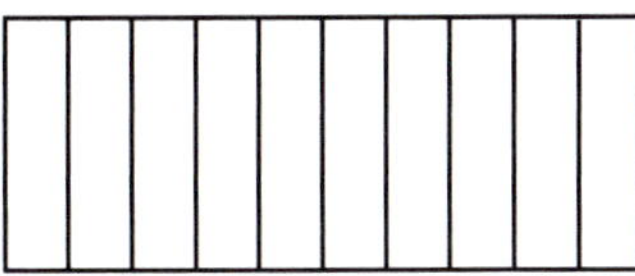

$\frac{2}{3}$

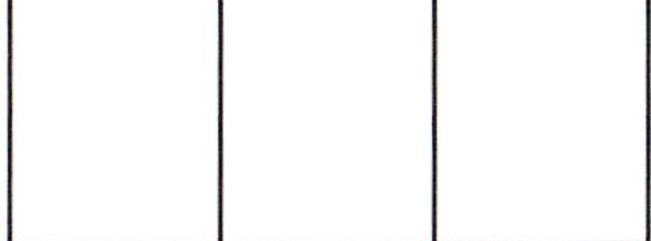

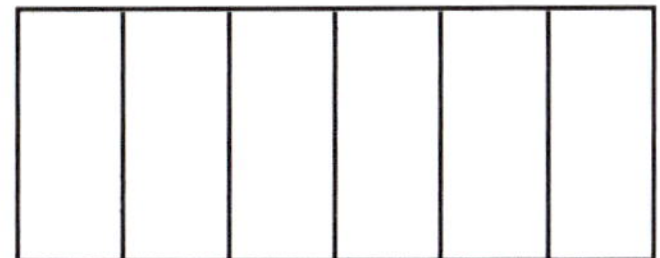

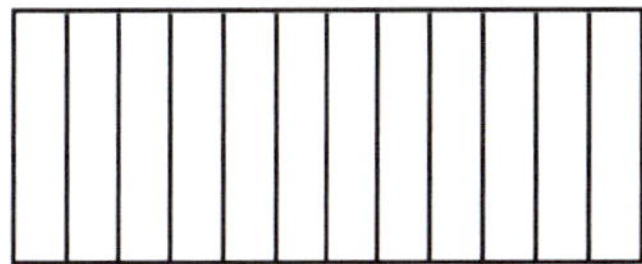

Shade the first diagram to show the fraction. Shade the second diagram to show an equivalent fraction.

$\frac{1}{8}$

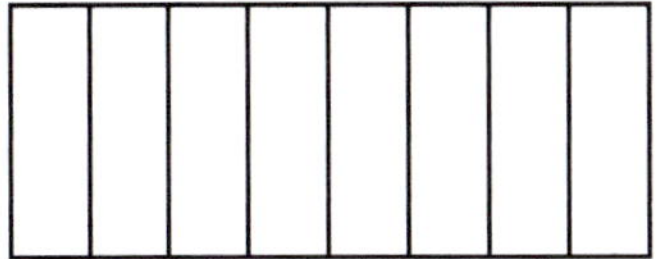

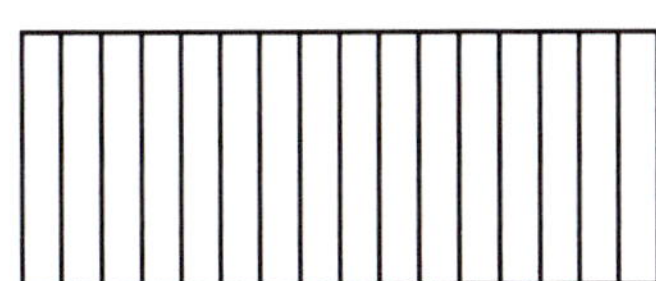

____

$\frac{3}{8}$

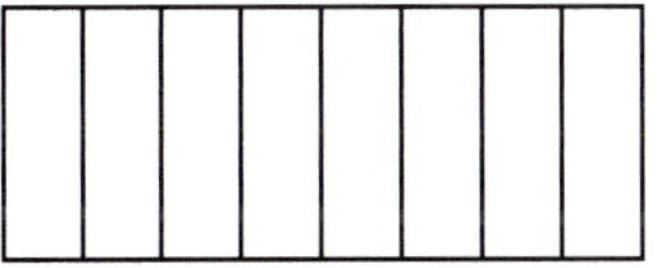

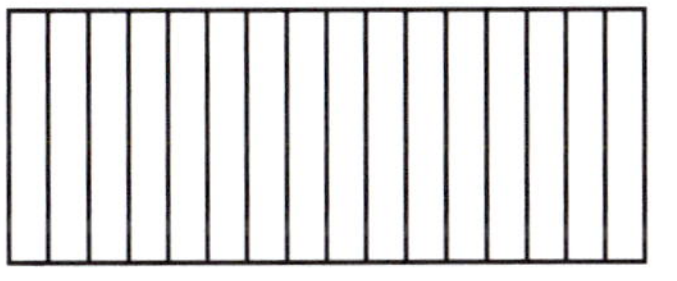

____

$\frac{2}{10}$

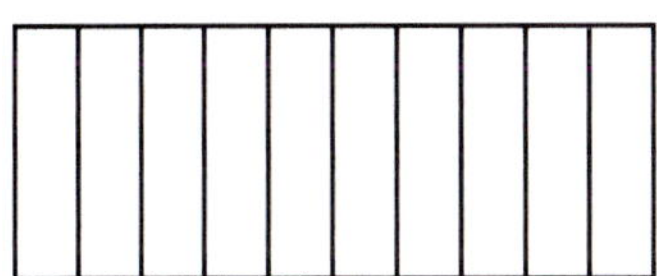

____

BOB time!

$\frac{7}{8}$

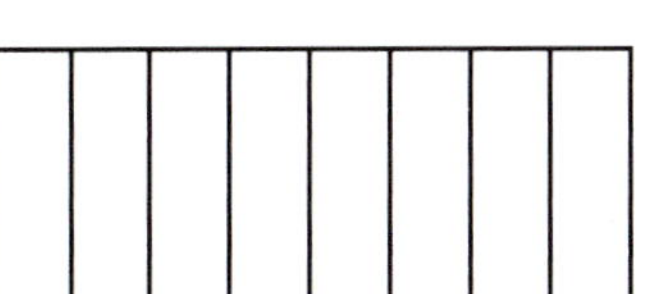

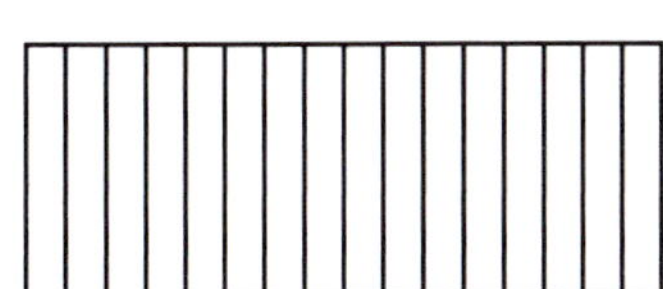

____

SUBTRACTING FRACTIONS

Notice that only the numerator changes. The denominator stays the same.

Counting back on a number line is a good way of subtracting one fraction from another.

To work out $\frac{5}{8} - \frac{3}{8}$, you can start on $\frac{5}{8}$ and count back three eighths ($\frac{4}{8}$, $\frac{3}{8}$, $\frac{2}{8}$). So the answer is $\frac{2}{8}$.

Look at this on the number line.

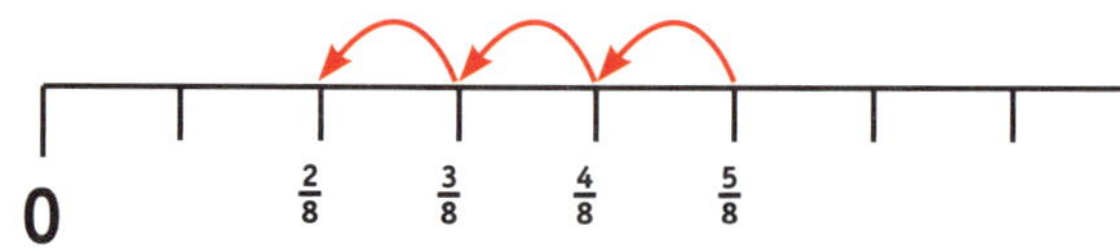

You can also subtract by **counting on**.

To work out $\frac{5}{8} - \frac{3}{8}$, start with the smaller fraction, $\frac{3}{8}$, and count on until you reach $\frac{5}{8}$.

There are only **two jumps** ($\frac{4}{8}$,$\frac{5}{8}$) so the answer is $\frac{2}{8}$.

Look at this on the number line.

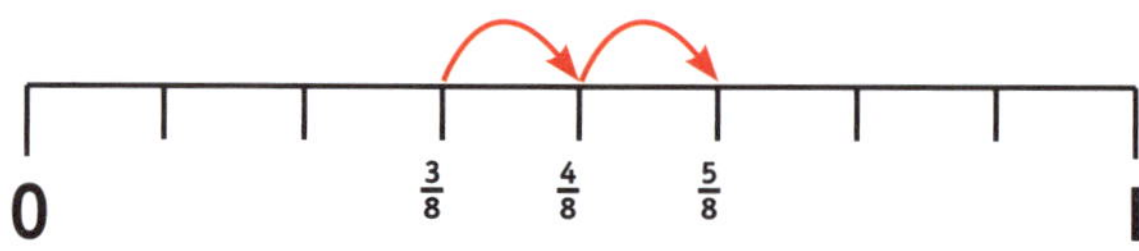

If you want to work out $\frac{1}{2} - \frac{2}{6}$, then you need to think about **equivalent fractions**. By changing the $\frac{1}{2}$ into sixths (you know $\frac{1}{2}$ is equivalent to $\frac{3}{6}$) you can show the subtraction on the number line by **counting back**.

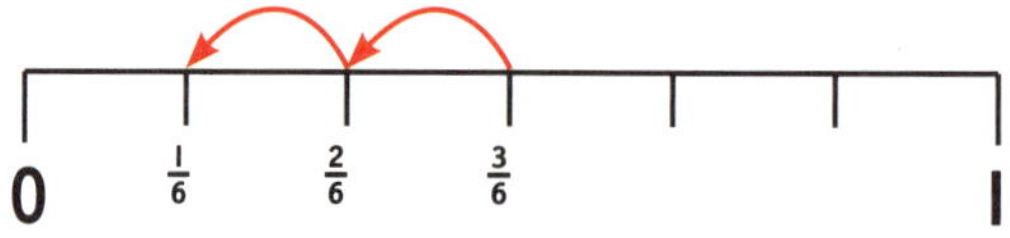

We practise

Work out $\frac{3}{4} - \frac{1}{4}$ by counting back on the number line.

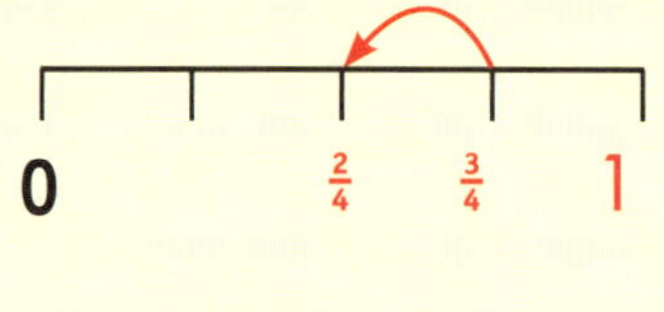

$\frac{3}{4} - \frac{1}{4} = \frac{2}{4}$ or $\frac{1}{2}$

Work out $\frac{2}{3} - \frac{1}{6}$ on the number line by counting on.

$\frac{2}{3}$ is equivalent to $\frac{4}{6}$.

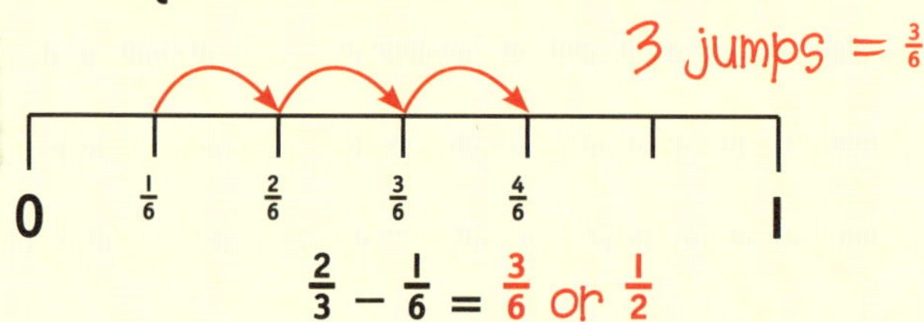

$\frac{2}{3} - \frac{1}{6} = \frac{3}{6}$ or $\frac{1}{2}$

You practise

Work out these subtractions by counting back on the number line.

1. $\frac{7}{8} - \frac{3}{8} =$ ____________ 0 ⎯⎯⎯⎯⎯ 1

2. $\frac{5}{6} - \frac{2}{6} =$ ____________ 0 ⎯⎯⎯⎯⎯ 1

3. $\frac{6}{10} - \frac{4}{10} =$ ____________ 0 ⎯⎯⎯⎯⎯ 1

4. $\frac{3}{5} - \frac{2}{5} =$ ____________ 0 ⎯⎯⎯⎯⎯ 1

5. $\frac{5}{8} - \frac{2}{8} =$ ____________ 0 ⎯⎯⎯⎯⎯ 1

You practise

Work out these subtractions by counting on using a number line.

6. $\frac{5}{8} - \frac{1}{2} =$ ____________ 0 ⎯⎯⎯⎯⎯ 1

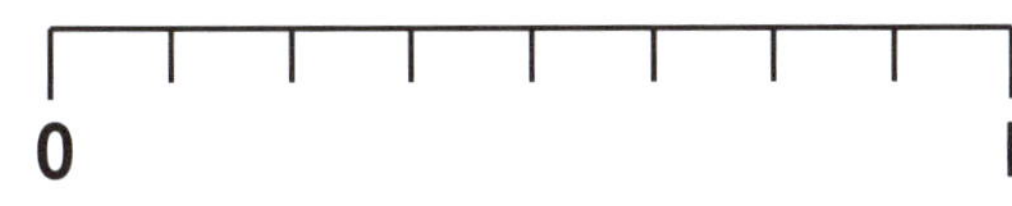

7. $\frac{3}{4} - \frac{1}{2} =$ ____________ 0 ⎯⎯⎯⎯⎯ 1

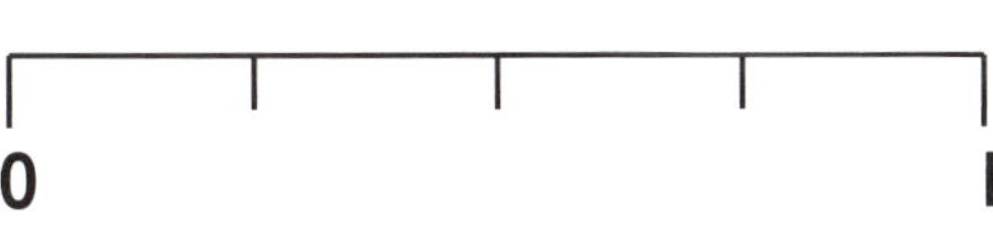

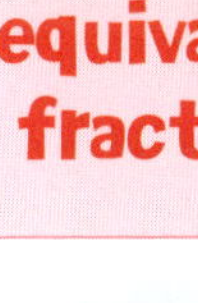

Remember, it helps to think of the equivalent fraction.

8. $\frac{1}{2} - \frac{1}{8} =$ ____________ 0 ⎯⎯⎯⎯⎯ 1

9. $\frac{1}{3} - \frac{2}{6} =$ ____________ 0 ⎯⎯⎯⎯⎯ 1

10. $\frac{1}{2} - \frac{3}{10} =$ ____________ 0 ⎯⎯⎯⎯⎯ 1

FRACTIONS of a QUANTITY

How do you work out $\frac{3}{4} \times 12$?

The best way to start is to read this as $\frac{3}{4}$ **of 12** and think of 12 as a **quantity**:

"I have eaten $\frac{3}{4}$ of my 12 cherries. How many cherries have I eaten?"

Drawing a **picture** can also help. Below are the 12 cherries split into 4 equal groups (or quarters).

You can see that there are 3 cherries in each quarter, so the answer is **$3 \times 3 = 9$.**

Now try one without using a picture.

$\frac{3}{8} \times$ **16** (read it as $\frac{3}{8}$ **of 16**)

Step 1 Work out what $\frac{1}{8}$ of 16 is.
$\frac{1}{8} \times 16 = 2$

Step 2 Multiply 2 by 3 to find out how many there are in $\frac{3}{8}$.
$3 \times 2 = 6$

Step 3 Write the complete number sentence.
$\frac{3}{8} \times 16 = 6$

We practise

Show the steps for finding $\frac{5}{6} \times 12$.

Step 1 $\frac{1}{6} \times 12 = 2$

Step 2 $5 \times 2 = 10$

Step 3 $\frac{5}{6} \times 12 = 10$

Show the steps for finding $\frac{2}{5} \times 20$.

Step 1 $\frac{1}{5} \times 20 = 4$

Step 2 $2 \times 4 = 8$

Step 3 $\frac{2}{5} \times 20 = 8$

You practise

Show the steps for finding the answer to each fraction multiplication question.

$\frac{3}{5} \times 20$

Step 1 ______________________

Step 2 ______________________

Step 3 ______________________

3

$\frac{5}{6} \times 12$

Step 1 ______________________

Step 2 ______________________

Step 3 ______________________

$\frac{3}{8} \times 24$

Step 1 ______________________

Step 2 ______________________

Step 3 ______________________

$\frac{2}{5} \times 15$

Step 1 ______________________

Step 2 ______________________

Step 3 ______________________

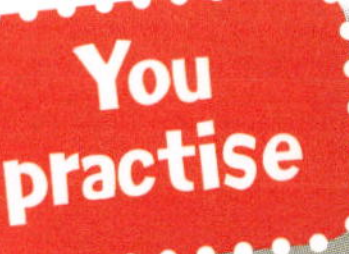

Think through first two steps and complete each fraction multiplication question.

$\frac{3}{8} \times 8 =$ ______________________

$\frac{4}{5} \times 10 =$ ______________________

$\frac{5}{8} \times 24 =$ ______________________

$\frac{3}{10} \times 40 =$ ______________________

BOB time!

FRACTIONS and MEASUREMENT

Fractions are used in lots of different **measurement** situations, including measuring **time**.

Knowing that there are 60 minutes in an hour helps with $\frac{1}{2}$ an hour (30 minutes), $\frac{1}{4}$ of an hour (15 minutes) and $\frac{3}{4}$ of an hour (45 minutes).

12 : 00 | 12 : 15 | 12 : 30 | 12 : 45

Capacity is another example where knowing fractional parts is essential.
Capacity is measured in either litres (L) or millilitres (mL).

1000 mL in 1 litre

750 mL in $\frac{3}{4}$ litre

500 mL in $\frac{1}{2}$ litre

250 mL in $\frac{1}{4}$ litre

We practise

What time will the clocks show in $\frac{3}{4}$ of an hour? Show the new time on the second clock faces.

12 : 15

1 : 00

Shade the jugs to show $1\frac{1}{4}$ litres of water.

How many millilitres in the jugs?

1250 mL

You practise Show the new time on each clock.

1 

In $\frac{1}{2}$ an hour it will be 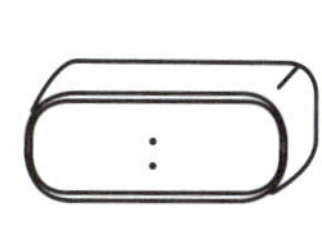

2 

In $\frac{3}{4}$ of an hour it will be 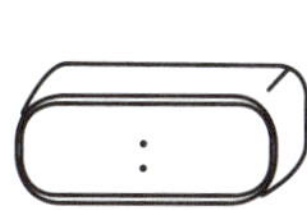

3 

$\frac{3}{4}$ of an hour ago it was 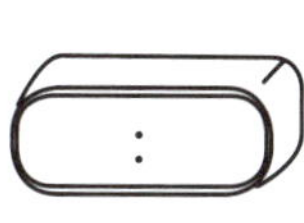

4 

$1\frac{1}{2}$ hours ago it was 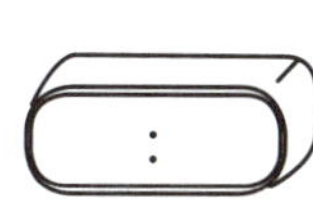

You practise Shade the jugs to match the amounts and write the equivalent measurements.

5 $1\frac{1}{4}$ litres 

= 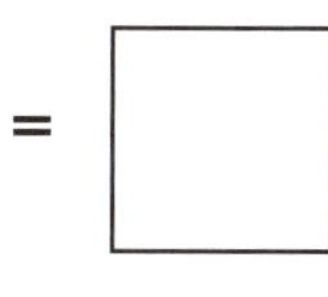

6 750 millilitres 

= 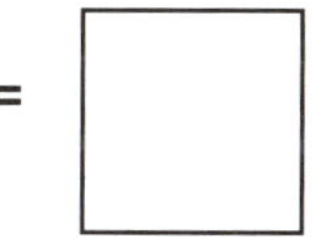

BOB time!

7 $\frac{3}{4}$ of a litre 

½ L =

8 1250 millilitres 

½ L ½ L =

PROBLEM SOLVING

Clare and Jake each have
an identical chocolate bar.
"Stop eating!" Mum says. "How much do you have left?"
she wants to know.
Clare says, "I have eaten $\frac{3}{4}$ of mine."
Jake says, "I have eaten 0·5 of mine."
"I need $\frac{5}{8}$ of a bar of chocolate for the cake. Do you have
enough left for me?" asks mum.

Remember to write the answer as a sentence.

Notice that the important information is highlighted in blue and what has to be found out is highlighted in pink.

Drawing the two chocolate bars split into eighths is one way of working out this problem.

Claire

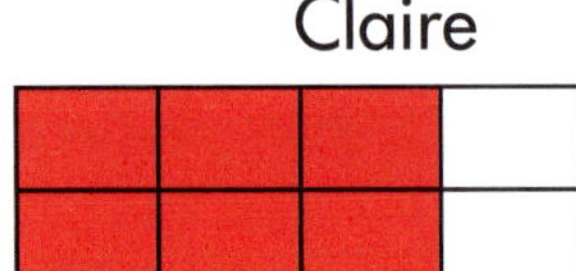

Jake

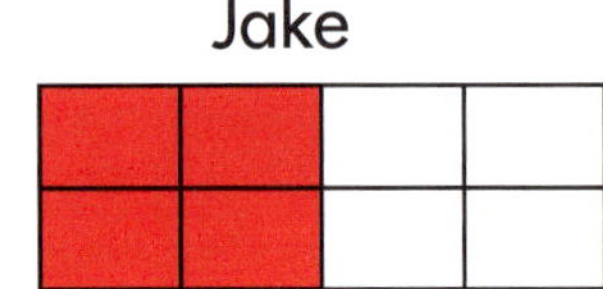

Use a number line to solve the problem.

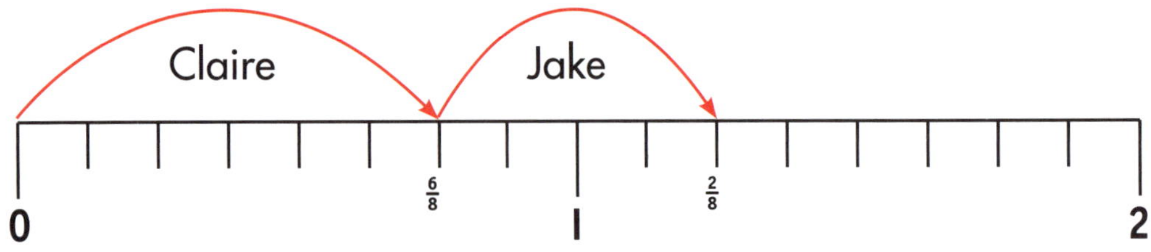

Answer: There is enough chocolate for Mum to make her cake.

We practise

Highlight the important information and what you have to find out in this problem.

To make the fancy dress costume 5 pieces of elastic are needed. One piece needs to be 0·6 of a metre. Two of the pieces need to be $\frac{1}{4}$ of a metre each. One piece needs to be 70 cm and the last piece has to be $\frac{3}{4}$ of a metre. How much elastic is needed? Use a number line to solve the problem.

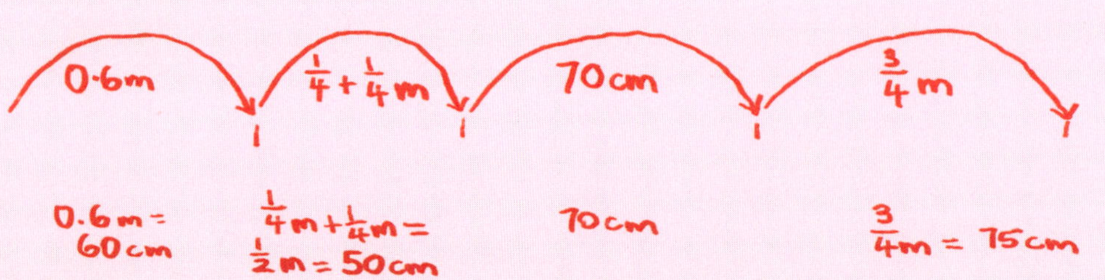

2·55 metres of elastic are needed.

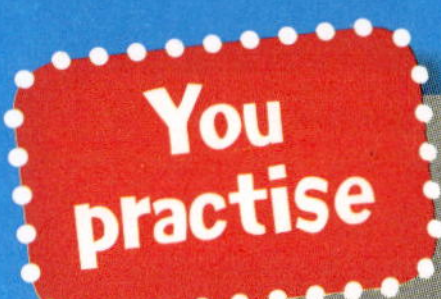

Highlight the important information and solve these problems.

1. The teacher prepared a bag of 20 blue, red and yellow counters for a game of chance. $\frac{3}{5}$ are blue and $\frac{1}{5}$ are red. How many are yellow? ____________

2. Clare ate $\frac{1}{4}$ of the lasagne, Jake ate $\frac{3}{16}$ and Tsai ate the rest. How much lasagne did Tsai eat? ____________

3. Put 0·58 and 0·66 in order on the number line.

   0·5 |———|———|———|———| 0·7

4. The soccer team has played 16 matches this season. They won $\frac{3}{8}$ and lost $\frac{1}{4}$ of the games. How many games did they draw? ____________

5. The tiler needs 36 large tiles for the bathroom. $\frac{1}{4}$ have to be black, $\frac{3}{6}$ white and the rest rust coloured. How many of each colour is that?

   ____

6. Clare left home at 8:15 am. She chatted to some friends for $\frac{1}{4}$ hour before walking the $\frac{1}{2}$-hour walk to school. School starts at 8:50am. How late was she?

   ____

7. There is a $\frac{1}{4}$-litre and a $\frac{1}{2}$-litre jug. Clare filled the jugs 4 times to make $1\frac{3}{4}$ litres. How many of each type of jug did she use?

   ____

8. Clare and Jake were playing with the fraction dice. At the end of 4 throws the player with a score closest to 2 wins the round. But they couldn't agree on who won.

   Clare threw $\frac{1}{2}$, $\frac{3}{8}$, $\frac{1}{4}$ and $\frac{5}{8}$ Jake threw $\frac{3}{4}$, $\frac{3}{8}$, $\frac{5}{8}$ and $\frac{1}{8}$

   Who won? ____________

9. Jake and Clare want to go to a movie that starts at 6:15pm and goes for $1\frac{1}{2}$ hours. It takes 15 minutes each way to walk to the cinema. What time should they leave home? ____________

   What time will they get home afterwards? ____________

10. The cordial mix should be $\frac{1}{5}$ cordial and $\frac{4}{5}$ water. How many mL of cordial are needed to make $\frac{1}{2}$L of drink? ____________

BOB time!

UNIT 11 DECIMALS to THOUSANDTHS

To mark 0·6 or $\frac{6}{10}$ on a **number line** you know that you have to mark the line in **tenths** and count to find out where 0·6 belongs.

The number line below is enlarged so that you can see the space between 0 and 0·1. Now you can see the **hundredths** between 0 and 0·1.

What's between 0 and 0·01?

Between 0 and 0·01 are **thousandths** – there are ten $\frac{1}{1000}$ between 0 and 0·01. In the number line below the arrow points to $\frac{3}{1000}$, which is written as 0·003.

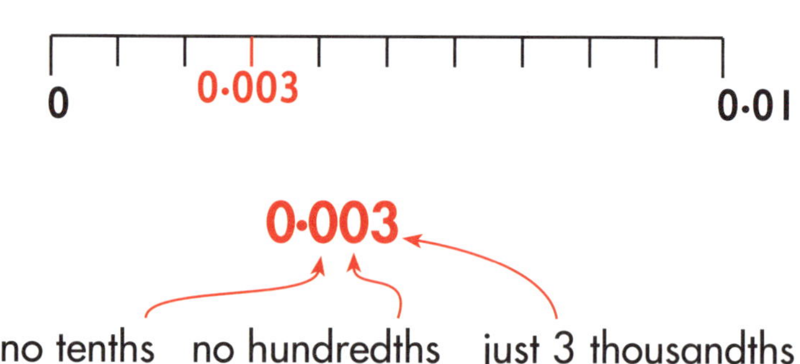

0·003

no tenths no hundredths just 3 thousandths

We practise

Mark 0·007 on this number line.

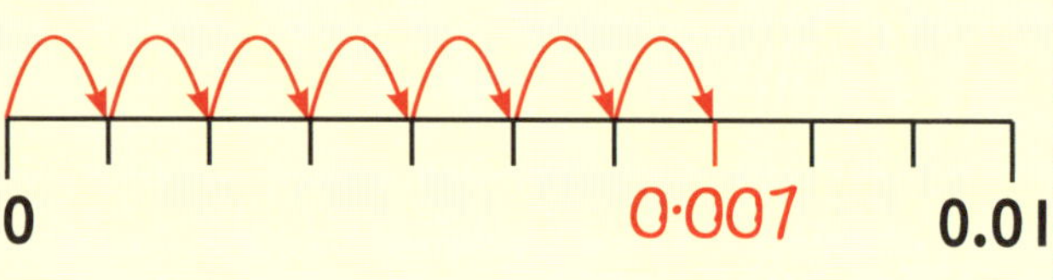

Write 0·007 as a fraction.

$\frac{7}{1000}$

What decimal fraction is shown on this number line?

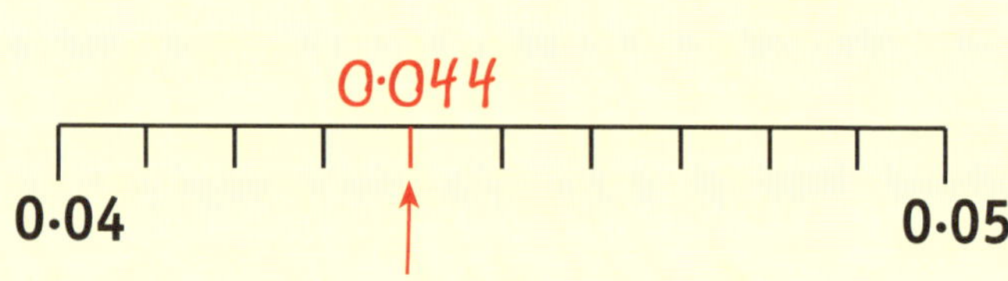

Write the decimal as a fraction.

$\frac{44}{1000}$

FRACTIONS & DECIMALS

YEARS 5 and 6

FRACTIONS & DECIMALS
YEARS 5 and 6
FRACTIONS & DECIMALS
YEARS 5 and 6
FRACTIONS & DECIMALS
YEARS 5 and 6
FRACTIONS & DECIMALS
YEARS 5 and 6
FRACTIONS & DECIMALS
YEARS 5 and 6
FRACTIONS & DECIMALS
YEARS 5 and 6
FRACTIONS & DECIMALS
YEARS 5 and 6
FRACTIONS & DECIMALS
YEARS 5 and 6
FRACTIONS & DECIMALS
YEARS 5 and 6
FRACTIONS & DECIMALS
YEARS 5 and 6
FRACTIONS & DECIMALS
YEARS 5 and 6
FRACTIONS & DECIMALS
YEARS 5 and 6
FRACTIONS & DECIMALS
YEARS 5 and 6
FRACTIONS & DECIMALS
YEARS 5 and 6
FRACTIONS & DECIMALS
YEARS 5 and 6

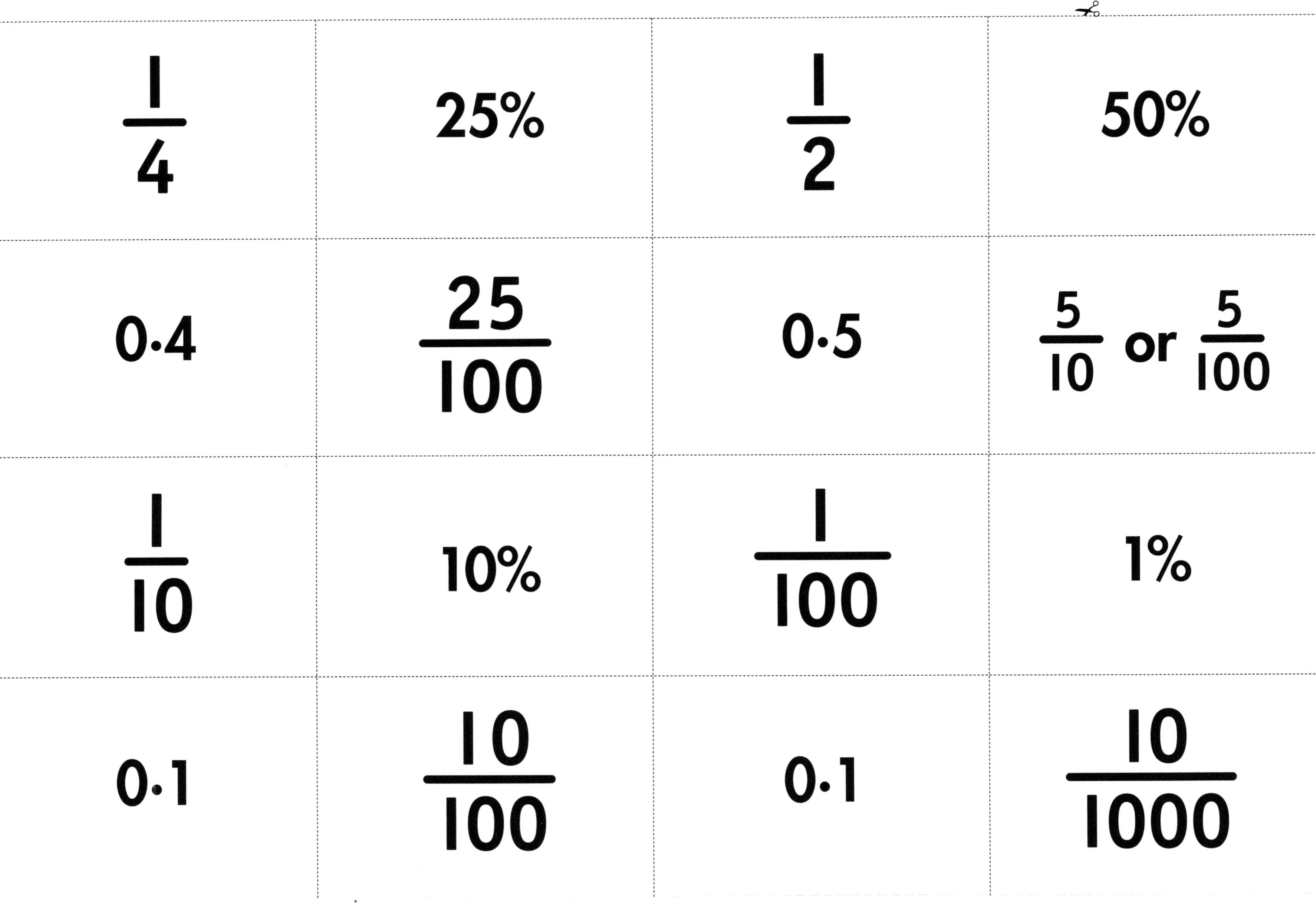

$\frac{1}{4}$	25%	$\frac{1}{2}$	50%
0·4	$\frac{25}{100}$	0·5	$\frac{5}{10}$ or $\frac{5}{100}$
$\frac{1}{10}$	10%	$\frac{1}{100}$	1%
0·1	$\frac{10}{100}$	0·1	$\frac{10}{1000}$

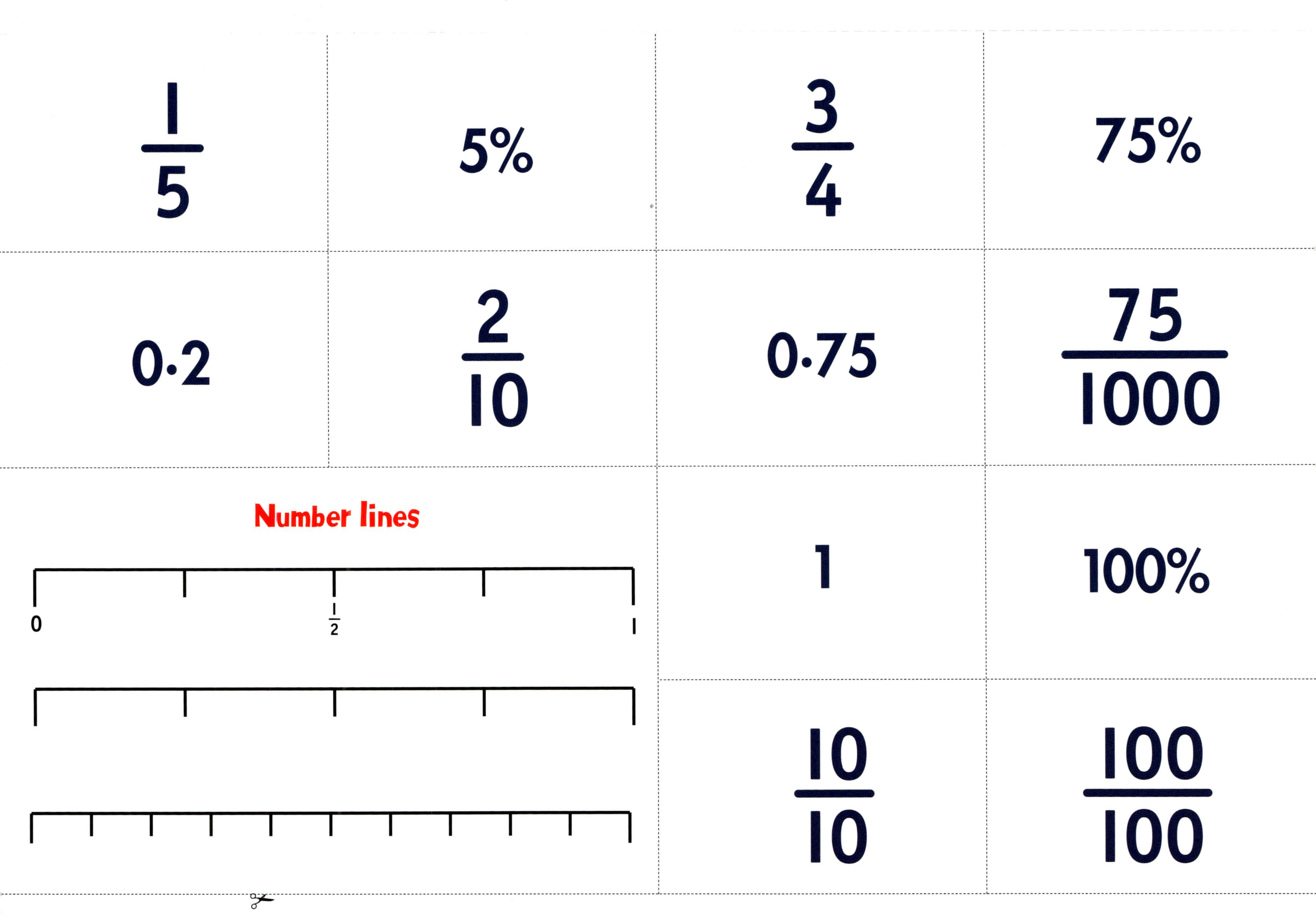

1/5
5%
3/4
75%
0·2
2/10
0·75
75/1000
Number lines
0
1/2
1
1
100%
10/10
100/100

Back to Basics

FRACTIONS & DECIMALS

YEARS 5 and 6

Back to Basics

FRACTIONS & DECIMALS

YEARS 5 and 6

Back to Basics

FRACTIONS & DECIMALS

YEARS 5 and 6

Back to Basics

FRACTIONS & DECIMALS

YEARS 5 and 6

Back to Basics

FRACTIONS & DECIMALS

YEARS 5 and 6

Back to Basics

FRACTIONS & DECIMALS

YEARS 5 and 6

Back to Basics

FRACTIONS & DECIMALS

YEARS 5 and 6

Back to Basics

FRACTIONS & DECIMALS

YEARS 5 and 6

Back to Basics

FRACTIONS & DECIMALS

YEARS 5 and 6

Back to Basics

FRACTIONS & DECIMALS

YEARS 5 and 6

Back to Basics

FRACTIONS & DECIMALS

YEARS 5 and 6

Back to Basics

FRACTIONS & DECIMALS

YEARS 5 and 6

Back to Basics

NUMBER LINES

YEARS 5 and 6

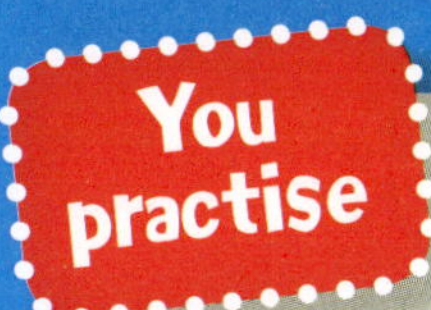

Mark the decimal on each number line and then write the decimal as a fraction.

Fraction

0·006

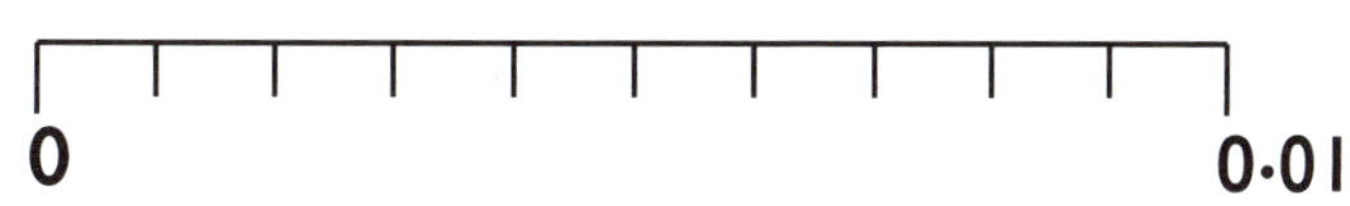

0·016

0·035

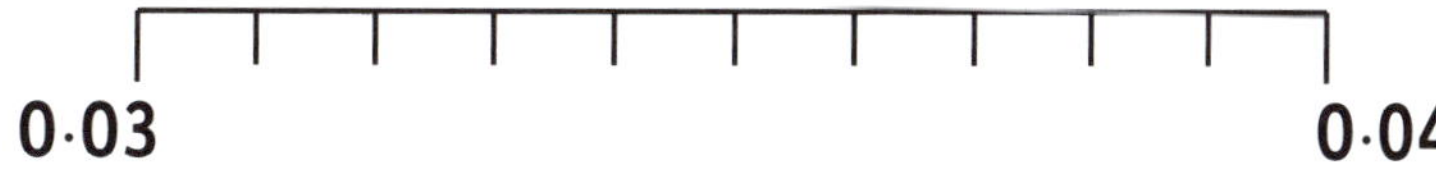

0·346

Write the decimal shown on the number line as a decimal and as a fraction.

Decimal | Fraction

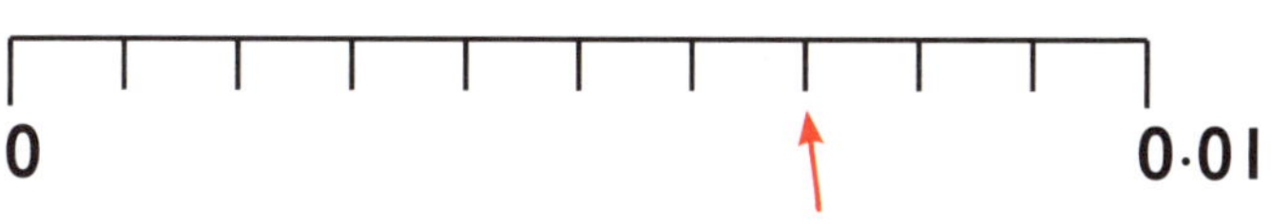

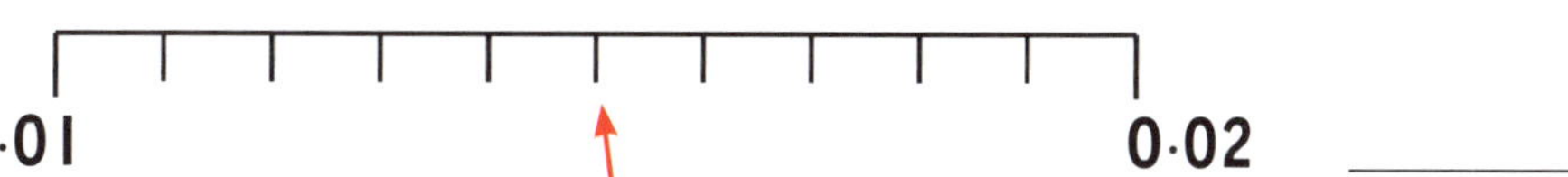

0·04 — 0·05

0·14 — 0·15

BOB time!

ROUNDING DECIMALS

Any number 5 or more rounds up, but any number 4 or less rounds down.

When you pay for something you sometimes need to round up or round down.

For an item that costs \$1·98, you need to **round up** to \$2 because there are no 2c coins.

For an item that costs \$1·92, you **round down** to \$1·90. And if an item costs \$1·48, you usually round to the nearest 5c, which is \$1·50.

You can round decimals too:

- 1·8 rounds up to the nearest whole number (2).
- 1·4 rounds down to the nearest whole number (1).
- 1·88 rounds up to the nearest tenth (1·9) or up to the nearest whole number (2).
- 1·82 rounds down the nearest tenth (1·8) or up to the nearest whole number (2).
- 1·888 rounds up to the nearest hundredth (1·89), the nearest tenth (1·9) or the nearest whole number (2).
- 1·882 rounds down to the nearest hundredth (1·88), up to the nearest tenth (1·9) or up to the nearest whole number (2).

Knowing how to round decimals is useful when doing operations with decimals.

We practise

Round 1·89 to the nearest tenth and then to the nearest whole number.

Nearest tenth: 1·9

Nearest whole number: 2

Round 1·344 to the nearest hundredth, tenth and whole number.

Nearest hundredth: 1·34

Nearest tenth: 1·3

Nearest whole number: 1

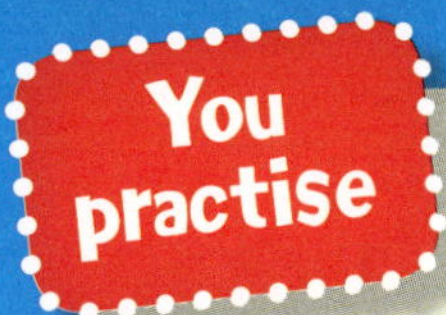

Round these decimal numbers to the nearest tenth and to the nearest whole number.

		Tenth	Whole number
1	1·79	______	______
2	3·56	______	______
3	3·49	______	______
4	6·72	______	______
5	8·64	______	______

You practise

Round these decimal numbers to the nearest hundredth, tenth and whole number.

		Hundredth	Tenth	Whole number
6	2·889	______	______	______
7	3·444	______	______	______
8	4·376	______	______	______
9	3·457	______	______	______
10	3·523	______	______	______

BOB time!

UNIT 13

ADDING and SUBTRACTING DECIMALS

It can be easy to make mistakes when **adding and subtracting decimals**. So before you begin, it is a good idea to **round up** or **down** to find an **estimate** that is close to the answer.

Look at these examples.

36·6	round 36·6 up to 37
+ 37·8	and 37·8 up to 38
	The answer will be close to, but less than, 75.
43·36	round 43·36 down to 43
− 17·92	and 17·92 up to 18
	The answer will be close to, but more than, 25.
27·369	round 27·369 down to 27
+ 16·256	and 16·256 down to 16
	The answer will be close to, but more than, 43.

Use a calculator to check these additions and subtractions.

An estimate is a good way to check that you have the correct answer.

We practise

Round these numbers to find an estimate for this addition:

$$\begin{array}{r} 43{\cdot}76 \\ +\ 27{\cdot}62 \end{array}$$

43·76 rounds up to 44
27·62 rounds up to 28

The answer will be close to, but less than, 72.

Round these numbers to find an estimate for this subtraction:

$$\begin{array}{r} 27{\cdot}853 \\ -\ 16{\cdot}133 \end{array}$$

27·853 rounds up to 28
16·1333 rounds down to 16

The answer will be close to, but less than, 12.

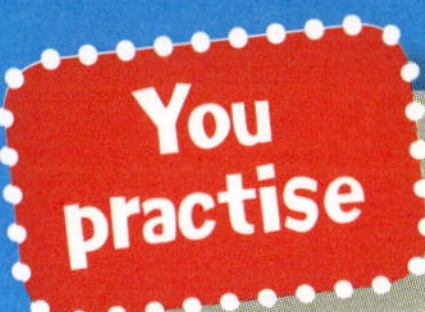

Round these numbers to find estimates for the actual answers.

36·7 rounds ________ to ________
+ 24·6 rounds ________ to ________
The answer will be close to, but ____________ than, ________

43·25 rounds ________ to ________
+ 47·36 rounds ________ to ________
The answer will be close to, but ____________ than, ________

32·95 rounds ________ to ________
− 17·05 rounds ________ to ________
The answer will be close to, but ____________ than, ________

34·72 rounds ________ to ________
− 17·38 rounds ________ to ________
The answer will be close to, but ____________ than, ________

13·769 rounds ________ to ________
+ 26·687 rounds ________ to ________
The answer will be close to, but ____________ than, ________

27·392 rounds ________ to ________
+ 36·899 rounds ________ to ________
The answer will be close to, but ____________ than, ________

36·108 rounds ________ to ________
− 19·576 rounds ________ to ________
The answer will be close to, but ____________ than, ________

8

99·765 rounds ________ to ________
− 49·988 rounds ________ to ________
The answer will be close to, but ____________ than, ________

BOB time!

USE THAT CALCULATOR

You know that $\frac{6}{10}$ is **equivalent** to 0·6, but what is $\frac{5}{8}$ equivalent to? To find out, you can use a **calculator**.

press **5** ÷ **8** = display shows **0·625**

What is $\frac{1}{3}$ is equivalent to?

press **1** ÷ **3** = display shows **0·33333333**

The 3s continue to the end of the calculator display and beyond.

Usually, you only need to read a decimal to **two decimal places**. So for $\frac{1}{3}$, you would say 0·33.

You can use a calculator to find equivalent decimals for fractions, such as $\frac{23}{3}$, simply by dividing the 23 by 3. This time you have a **whole number** and a **decimal part**.

press **23** ÷ **3** = display shows **7·66666666**

You need to **round up** to two decimal places, which means that the answer is 7·67.

When you are rounding to two decimals places, if the next decimal place value is 5 or more, then round up by 1.

We practise

Use your calculator to find $\frac{4}{7}$ as a decimal.

Press 4 ÷ 7 =

Display shows 0·57142857

Write the answer to two decimal places:

0·57

Use your calculator to find $\frac{23}{6}$ as decimal.

Press 23 ÷ 6 =

Display shows 3·8333333

Write the answer to two decimal places:

3·83

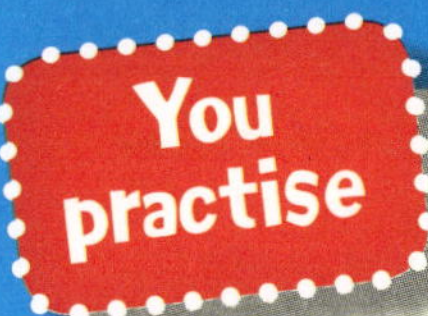

Use your calculator to find the decimal equivalents for these fractions.

 $\frac{7}{8}$ ________

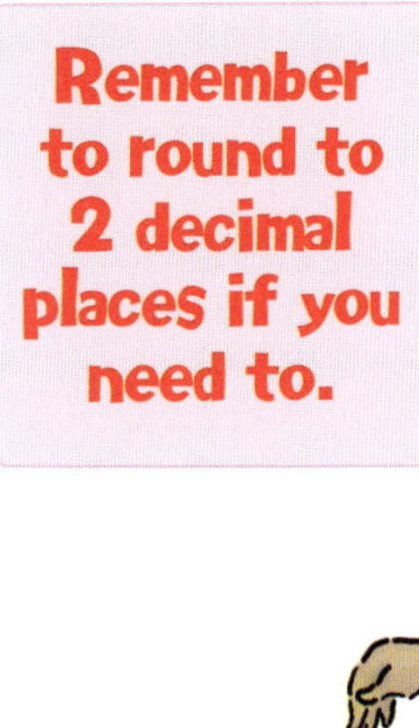

 $\frac{4}{5}$ ________

 $\frac{5}{8}$ ________

 $\frac{4}{6}$ ________

 $\frac{7}{9}$ ________

 $\frac{15}{6}$ ________

 $\frac{42}{6}$ ________

 $\frac{31}{6}$ ________

 $\frac{33}{8}$ ________

 $\frac{25}{7}$ ________

BOB time!

MULTIPLYING DECIMALS

Number splitting means dealing with each place value part separately.

Rounding and **adjusting** is a strategy that you can use for **multiplying decimals**. Look at these steps.

3 × 1·95

Step 1 Round \$1·95 up to \$2 3 × \$2 = \$6

Step 2 You know that \$2 is 5c too much 3 × 5c = 15c

Step 3 \$6 – 15c = \$5·85

Number splitting is another useful strategy.

2·65 × 4

Step 1 Find the close answer by working out 4 × 2 = 8. So the answer is close to, but greater than, 8.

Step 2 Find 4 lots of 0·6 or $\frac{6}{10} \times 4 = \frac{24}{10}$, which is equivalent to 2·4.

Step 3 Find 4 lots of 0·05 or $\frac{5}{100} \times 4 = \frac{20}{100}$, which is equivalent to 0·2.

Step 4 Add the amounts together to find the answer:

8 + 2·4 + 0·2

10 + 0·6

10·6

We practise

Solve this multiplication by rounding and adjusting.

4 × 3·85

Step 1 4 × 4 = 16

Step 2 4 × 0·15 = 0·6

Step 3 16 – 0·6 = 15·4

Solve this multiplication by number splitting.

3·56 × 3

Step 1 3 × 3 = 9

Step 2 $3 \times 0·5 = 3 \times \frac{5}{10} = \frac{15}{10} = 1·5$

Step 3 $3 \times 0·06 = 3 \times \frac{6}{100} = \frac{18}{100} = 0·18$

Step 4 9 + 1·5 + 0·18 = 10·68

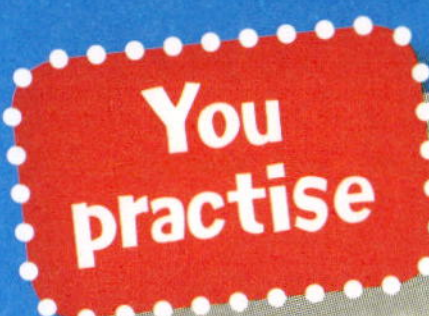

Solve these multiplications by rounding and adjusting.

1. $3 \times 2{\cdot}99$

Step 1 ______________________

Step 2 ______________________

Step 3 ______________________

2. $5 \times 3{\cdot}75$

Step 1 ______________________

Step 2 ______________________

Step 3 ______________________

3. $3 \times 4{\cdot}09$

Step 1 ______________________

Step 2 ______________________

Step 3 ______________________

Thinking about a related money question might help.

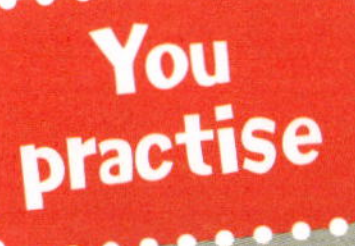

Use number splitting to solve these multiplication questions.

4. $4{\cdot}55 \times 4$

Step 1 ______________________

Step 2 ______________________

Step 3 ______________________

Step 4 ______________________

5. $3{\cdot}36 \times 3$

Step 1 ______________________

Step 2 ______________________

Step 3 ______________________

Step 4 ______________________

6. $5{\cdot}17 \times 3$

Step 1 ______________________

Step 2 ______________________

Step 3 ______________________

Step 4 ______________________

MULTIPLYING and DIVIDING BY 10s and 100s

Working with whole numbers is sometimes easier when multiplying and dividing decimals.

To change 0·036 into a whole number, you could multiply by 10, then by 10 again and then by 10 again. Look at these steps.

0·036 × 10 = 0·36

0·36 × 10 = 3·6

3·6 × 10 = 36

It would be **quicker** to simply **multiply by 1000**, which is the same as 10 × 10 × 10.

Use your calculator to follow these steps.

So repeatedly **multiplying by 10** changes a decimal number into a whole number, but **dividing by 10** has the opposite effect.

36 ÷ 10 = 3·6

3·6 ÷ 10 = 0·36

0·36 ÷ 10 = 0·036

It would be **quicker** to simply **divide by 1000**.

We practise

Change 0·43 into 43 by multiplying by 10s. Then use the quickest method.

0·43 × 10 = 4·3
4·3 × 10 = 43

or

0·43 × 100 = 43

Change 345 into 0·345 by dividing by 10s. Then use the quickest method.

345 ÷ 10 = 34·5
34·5 ÷ 10 = 3·45
3·45 ÷ 10 = 0·345

or

345 ÷ 1000 = 0·345

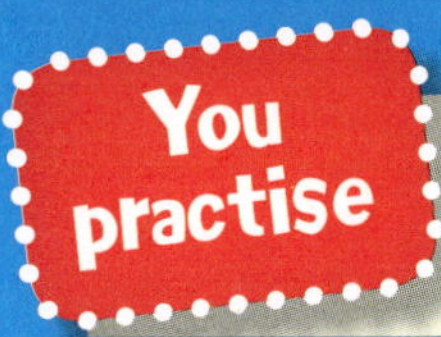

Change these decimals into whole numbers using the quickest method.

1 4·9 ______________________________

2 3·67 ______________________________

3 4·08 ______________________________

4 5·679 ______________________________

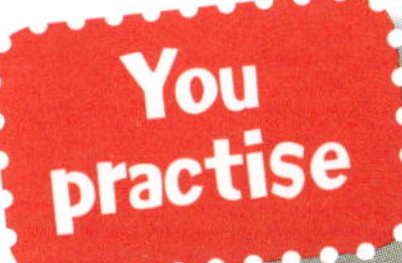

Change these whole numbers into decimal numbers less than 1 using the quickest method.

5 36 ______________________________

6 15 ______________________________

7 325 ______________________________

8 4 563 ______________________________

MULTIPLYING FRACTIONS and DECIMALS

When you **multiply a fraction**, such as $\frac{3}{4} \times 2$, it actually means **$\frac{3}{4}$ of a group of 2**. This diagram makes it easy to understand.

$\frac{3}{4}$ 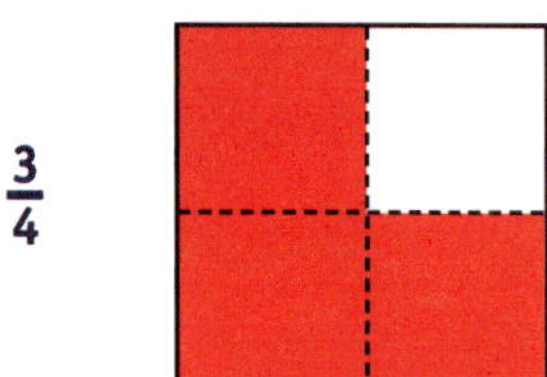 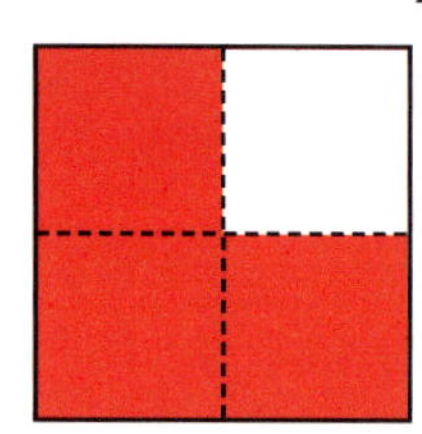 $\frac{3}{4}$

The diagram shows that $\frac{3}{4} \times 2 = \frac{6}{4}$, and you know that $\frac{6}{4}$ is **equivalent** to $1\frac{1}{2}$.

$$\frac{3}{4} \times 2 = \frac{6}{4} = 1\frac{1}{2}$$

You can also use fractions to help you **multiply by decimals**. $\frac{3}{4}$ is equivalent to 0·75, so $\frac{3}{4} \times 2$ could also be written as 0·75 × 2.

Here's a good way to think about multiplying fractions. Write the number 2 as a fraction, $\frac{2}{1}$.

$$\frac{3}{4} \times \frac{2}{1}$$

Now multiply the numerators (3 x 2 = 6) and multiply the denominators (4 × 1 = 4). So the complete number sentence is:

$$\frac{3}{4} \times \frac{2}{1} = \frac{6}{4} = 1\frac{1}{2}$$

We practise

Shade the diagrams to show $\frac{3}{8} \times 2$.

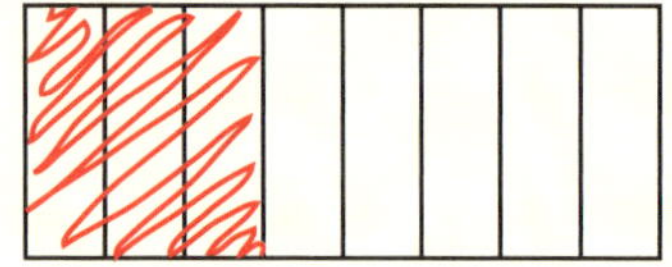 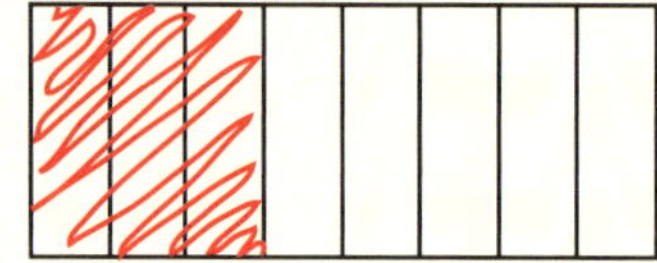

Write $\frac{3}{8} \times \frac{2}{1}$ as a number sentence.

$\frac{3}{8} \times \frac{2}{1} = \frac{6}{8}$ or $\frac{3}{4}$

Write the multiplication as a number sentence.

$\frac{4}{5} \times 3$

$\frac{4}{5} \times \frac{3}{1} = \frac{12}{5} = 2\frac{2}{5}$

You practise Shade each diagram to show the multiplication. What is the answer?

$\frac{2}{3} \times 3$ 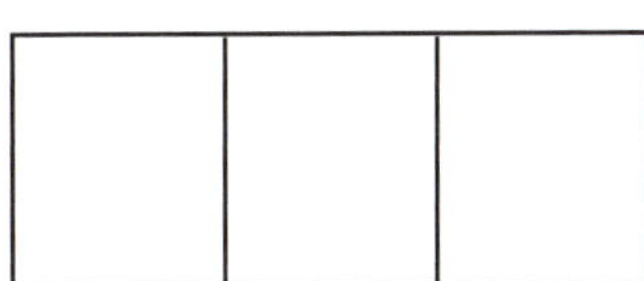 = ____

$\frac{3}{5} \times 2$ 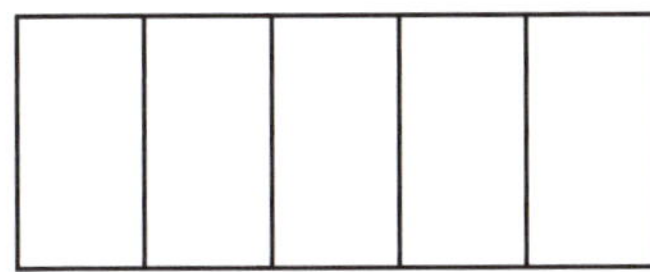 = ____

$\frac{3}{4} \times 3$ 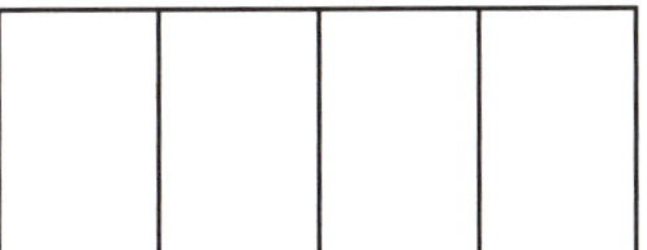 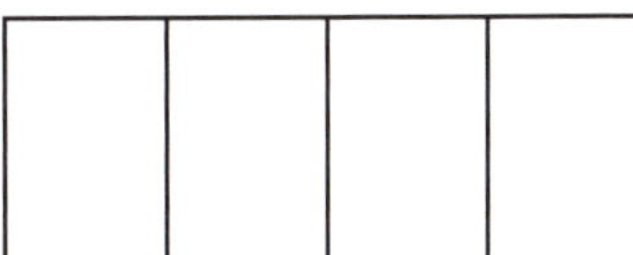 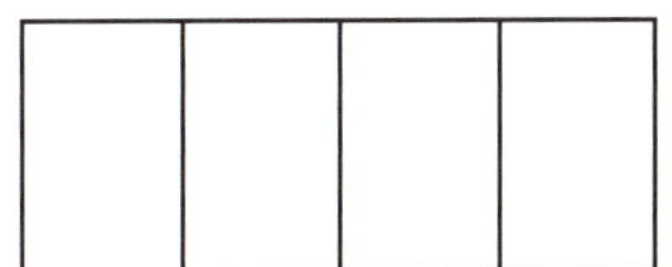 = ____

Complete the number sentences for these multiplications.

$\frac{1}{2} \times 8 =$ ____ × ____ = ____ = ____

$\frac{4}{5} \times 4 =$ ____ × ____ = ____ = ____

$\frac{2}{3} \times 6 =$ ____ × ____ = ____ = ____

$\frac{1}{4} \times 4 =$ ____ × ____ = ____ = ____

$\frac{7}{8} \times 3 =$ ____ × ____ = ____ = ____

DIVISION WITH DECIMALS

Multiplying decimals by 10s can help with division as well as with multiplication.

To solve **28 ÷ 0·4** you can **multiply** both the **whole number** and the **decimal number** by **10**.

Here are the steps.

Step 1 28 × 10 = 280 and 0·4 × 10 = 4

Step 2 280 ÷ 4 = 70

Because both numbers have been increased 10 times, the answer for the division is still the same.

Try it both ways on your calculator just to be sure.

Did you notice that the answer is larger than the number being divided?

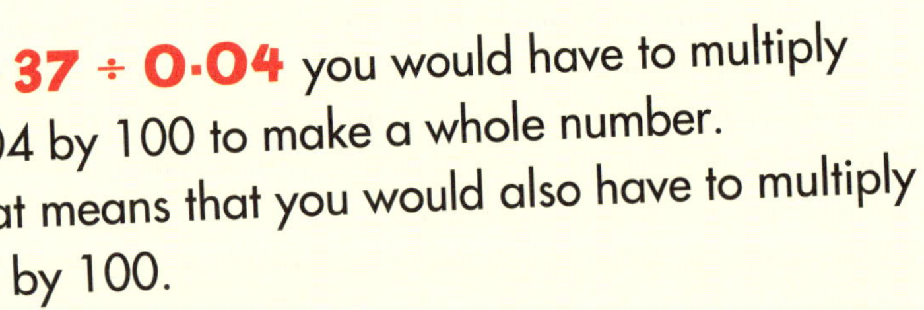

For **37 ÷ 0·04** you would have to multiply 0·04 by 100 to make a whole number.
That means that you would also have to multiply 37 by 100.

Here are the steps.

Step 1 37 × 100 = 3700 and 0·04 × 100 = 4

Step 2 3700 ÷ 4 = 925

We practise

Show the steps to solve this division:

48 ÷ 0·8

Step 1 48 × 10 = 480 and 0·8 × 10 = 8

Step 2 480 ÷ 8 = 60

Show the steps to solve this division:

35 ÷ 0·07

Step 1 35 × 100 = 3500 and 0·07 × 100 = 7

Step 2 3500 ÷ 7 = 500

You practise — Show the steps for solving these division questions

36 ÷ 0·9

Step 1 ________________ and ________________

Step 2 ________________

35 ÷ 0·7

Step 1 ________________ and ________________

Step 2 ________________

36 ÷ 0·4

Step 1 ________________ and ________________

Step 2 ________________

63 ÷ 0·7

Step 1 ________________ and ________________

Step 2 ________________

56 ÷ 0·07

Step 1 ________________ and ________________

Step 2 ________________

81 ÷ 0·09

Step 1 ________________ and ________________

Step 2 ________________

MENTAL MULTIPLICATION OF DECIMALS

To solve 36 × 0·4, you can multiply the decimal by 10 to make the whole number 4.

You know that 4 × 36 is 144, but that answer is 10 times too big.

You got this answer by multiplying by 10, so now you need to reverse this by dividing by 10.

Look at these steps.

Step 1 Multiply the decimal number by 10 to get a whole number.

0·4 × 10 = 4

Step 2 Then multiply 36 × 4 = 144

Step 3 Undo the multiplication by dividing by 10 to find the actual answer.

144 ÷ 10 = 14·4

Let's do another one.

27 × 0·3

Step 1 0·3 × 10 = 3

Step 2 27 × 3 = 81

Step 3 81 ÷ 10 = 8·1

We practise

Show the steps to solve these multiplications.

22 × 0·7

Step 1 0·7 × 10 = 7

Step 2 22 × 7 = 154

Step 3 154 ÷ 10 = 15·4

36 × 0·11

Step 1 0·11 × 100 = 11

Step 2 11 × 36 = 396

Step 3 396 ÷ 100 = 3·96

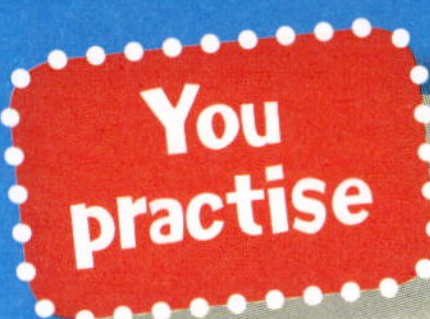

Show the steps for solving these multiplication questions.

32 × 0·8

Step 1 ______________________

Step 2 ______________________

Step 3 ______________________

36 × 0·5

Step 1 ______________________

Step 2 ______________________

Step 3 ______________________

27 × 0·9

Step 1 ______________________

Step 2 ______________________

Step 3 ______________________

0·8 × 24

Step 1 ______________________

Step 2 ______________________

Step 3 ______________________

5

0·7 × 35

Step 1 ______________________

Step 2 ______________________

Step 3 ______________________

Remember to check your answers with a calculator.

37 × 0·12

Step 1 ______________________

Step 2 ______________________

Step 3 ______________________

42 × 0·14

Step 1 ______________________

Step 2 ______________________

Step 3 ______________________

BOB time!

UNIT 20

PERCENTAGES

With these at your fingertips, it's easy to work out other percentages.

A percentage is another term for a hundredth.

A percentage is written using the symbol %.
You say 50% as 50 percent, which means 50 out of every hundred.

Below are some easy percentages.

1%	1 out of a hundred is equivalent to 0·01	To find 1% divide by 100	1% of 100 is 1
10%	10 out of a hundred is equivalent to 0·1	To find 10% divide by 10	10% of 100 is 10
25%	25 out of 100 is equivalent to 0·25 or $\frac{1}{4}$	To find 25% divide by 4	25% of 100 is 25
50%	50 out of 100 is equivalent to 0·5 or $\frac{1}{2}$	To find 50% divide by 2	50% of 100 is 50

To find **12% of 160** use these steps:

Step 1 Find 10% of 160 = 16 (divide by 10)
Step 2 Then find 1% of 160 = 1·6 (divide by 100)
Step 3 Then find 1% of 160 = 1·6 (divide by 100)
Step 4 Then add 16 + 1·6 + 1·6 = 19·2
12% of 160 = 19·2

We practise

Find 10% of 25 using an equivalent fraction.

$\frac{1}{10} \times 25 = 2{\cdot}5$

Find 25% of 120 using an equivalent fraction.

$\frac{1}{4} \times 120 = 30$

Find 13% of 160 using easy percentages.

Step 1 10% of 160 = 16
Step 2 1% of 150 = 1·6
Step 3 2% of 160 = 3·2
Step 4 16 + 1·6 + 3·2 = 20·8
13% of 160 = 20·8

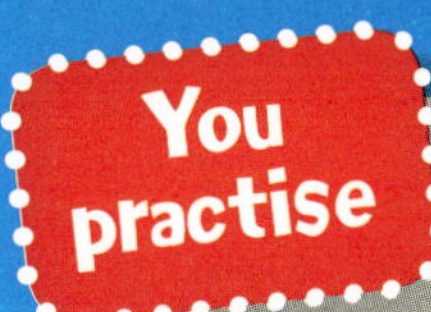

Show how to find each amount using equivalent fractions.

10% of 135 ________ × ________ = ________

1% of 135 ________ × ________ = ________

50% of 168 ________ × ________ = ________

10% of 75 ________ × ________ = ________

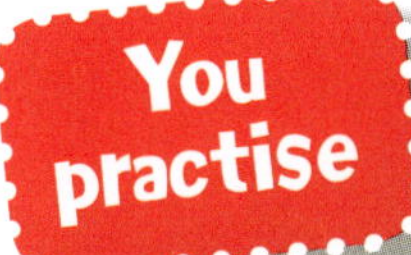

Show how to find each amount using easy percentages.

11% of 200

Step 1 ________

Step 2 ________

Step 3 ________

21% of 200

Step 1 ________

Step 2 ________

Step 3 ________

7 15% of 200

Step 1 ________

Step 2 ________

Step 3 ________

8 22% of 200

Step 1 ________

Step 2 ________

Step 3 ________

BOB time!

TEST 1

1 Use these number lines to show which is larger, $\frac{3}{8}$ or $\frac{2}{5}$.

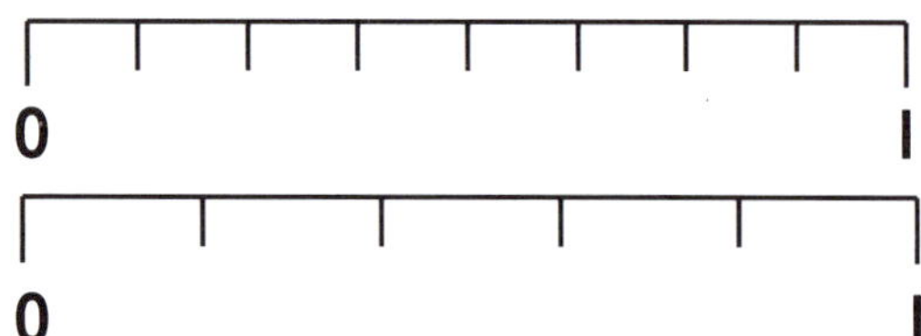

2 Write the equivalent fractions for this diagram.

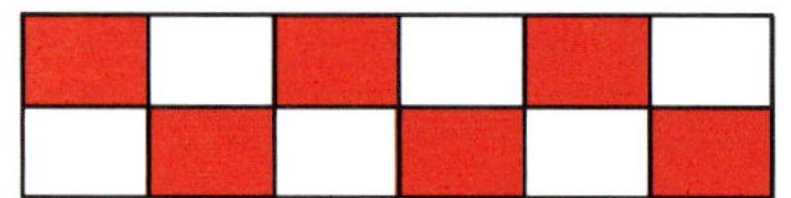

________ or ________

3 Show how to add these fractions using the open number line.

0 1 2

$\frac{5}{6} + \frac{1}{3} =$ ________

4 Write the decimal number and equivalent fractions for this diagram.

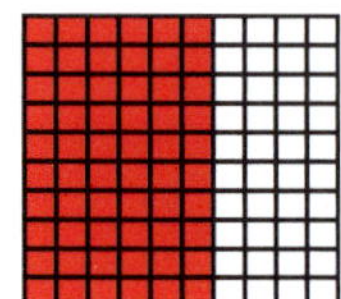

________ or ________ or ________

5 Order these decimal numbers on the number line. 0·6, 0·35, 0·7, 0·38

6 Shade and label the diagrams to show the equivalent fractions.

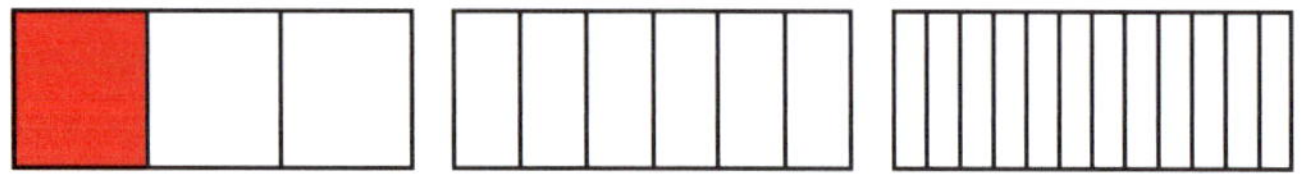

________ ________ ________

7 Show this fraction subtraction on a number line. $\frac{3}{4} - \frac{3}{8}$

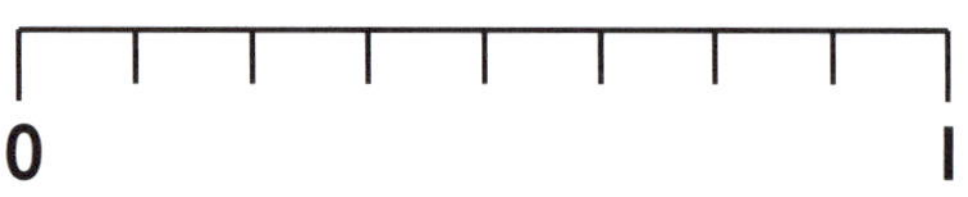

8 What is $\frac{3}{8} \times 32$? Step 1 ____________ Step 2 ____________

Step 3 ____________

9 It is now 6:45pm. What time will the clocks show in $1\frac{3}{4}$ hours time?

10 Shade the jugs to show $1\frac{3}{4}$ L of water.

TEST 2

Show where 0·056 is on the number line.

0·05 ——————————— 0·06

Round these decimals to the nearest whole number:

9·96 ____________

8·876 ____________

8·339 ____________

Round and find the estimated answer to:

13·768 rounds ______ to ______

+ 36·576 rounds ______ to ______

The answer will be close to, but ______ than, ______

Use your calculator to find the equivalent decimal for $\frac{5}{8}$. ______

Solve this multiplication by rounding and adjusting.

5 × 6·89 Step 1 ____________ Step 2 ____________

Show how to change these decimal numbers into whole numbers:

0·36 × ______ = ______ 0·488 × ______ = ______

Show how to solve $\frac{2}{3}$ × 12 = ______ × ______ = ______ = ______

Complete the number sentences for this multiplication:

33 × 0·3 Step 1 ____________

Step 2 ____________

Step 3 ____________

Show the steps for solving this division question:

54 ÷ 0·9 Step 1 ____________

Step 2 ____________

Step 3 ____________

What is 10% of 250? ______

ANSWERS

Unit 1

1
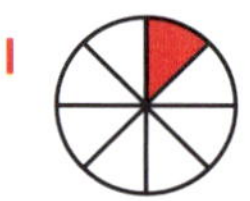

2 $\frac{1}{3}$
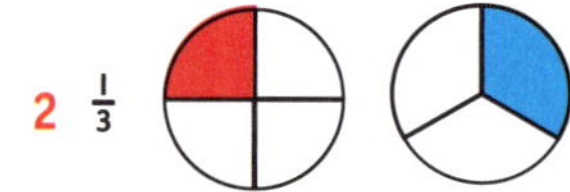

3 $\frac{5}{8}$

4

5 $\frac{1}{10}$, 4

6

Unit 2

1 $\frac{4}{8}$ is equivalent to $\frac{1}{2}$

2 $\frac{5}{10}$ is equivalent to $\frac{1}{2}$

3 $\frac{2}{6}$ is equivalent to $\frac{1}{3}$

4 $\frac{2}{8}$ is equivalent to $\frac{1}{4}$

5 $\frac{4}{8}$

6 $\frac{2}{8}$

7 $\frac{5}{10}$

8 $\frac{6}{12}$

Unit 3

1 1

2 $\frac{6}{8}$ or $\frac{3}{4}$
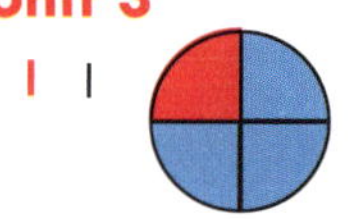

3 1

4 $\frac{5}{8}$
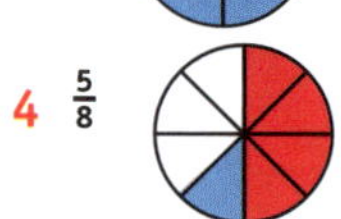

5 $\frac{4}{6}$ or $\frac{2}{3}$

6 $\frac{3}{4}$

0 $\frac{1}{2}$ $\frac{3}{4}$ 1

7 1

0 $\frac{1}{4}$ 1

8 $\frac{7}{8}$

0 $\frac{1}{8}$ $\frac{7}{8}$ 1

9 $\frac{3}{8}$

0 $\frac{1}{4}$ $\frac{3}{8}$ 1

10 $\frac{4}{6}$ or $\frac{2}{3}$

0 $\frac{1}{2}$ $\frac{4}{6}$ 1

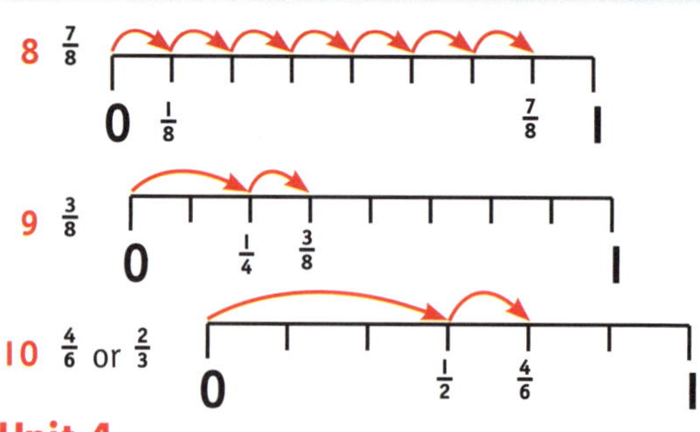

Unit 4

1 $\frac{6}{10}$ $\frac{60}{100}$ 0·6

2 $\frac{3}{10}$ $\frac{30}{100}$ 0·3

3 $\frac{11}{10}$ $\frac{110}{100}$ 1·1

4 $\frac{16}{10}$ $\frac{160}{100}$ 1·6

5 $\frac{50}{100}$ 0·5

6 $\frac{100}{100}$ 1

7 $\frac{120}{100}$ 1·2

8 $\frac{150}{100}$ 1·5

Unit 5

1 0·7 is larger than 0·35

2 0·75 is larger than 0·45

3 0·3 is larger than 0·03

4 0·8 is larger than 0·08

5 0 0·37 0·7 0·75 1

6 0 0·36 0·55 0·6 1

7 0 0·75 0·8 0·89 1

8 0 0·4 0·45 0·54 1

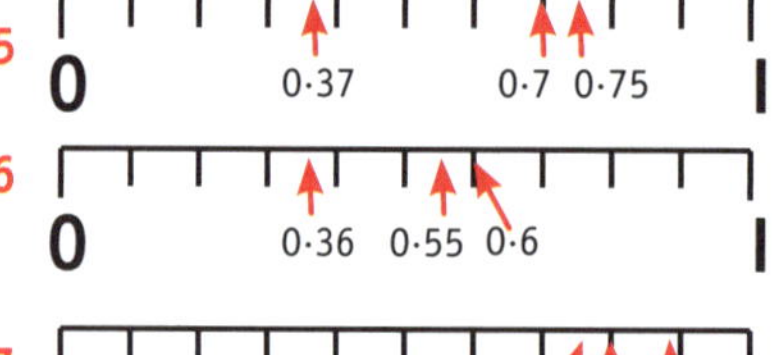

ANSWERS

Unit 6

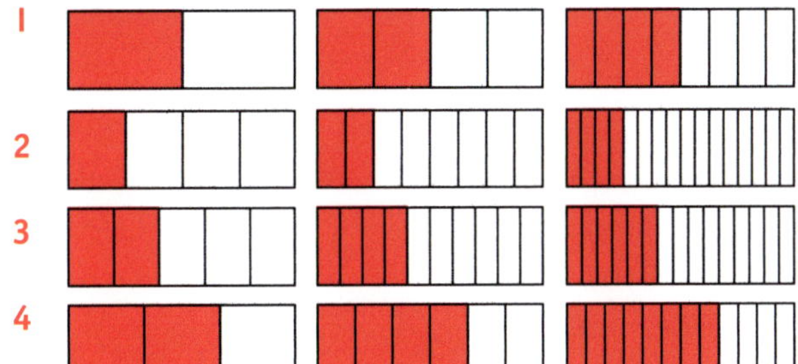

1

2

3

4

5 $\frac{2}{16}$

6 $\frac{6}{16}$

7 $\frac{4}{20}$

8 $\frac{14}{16}$

Unit 7

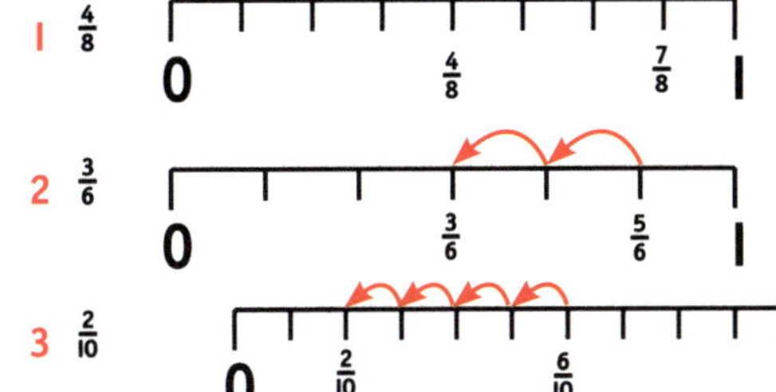

1 $\frac{4}{8}$

2 $\frac{3}{6}$

3 $\frac{2}{10}$

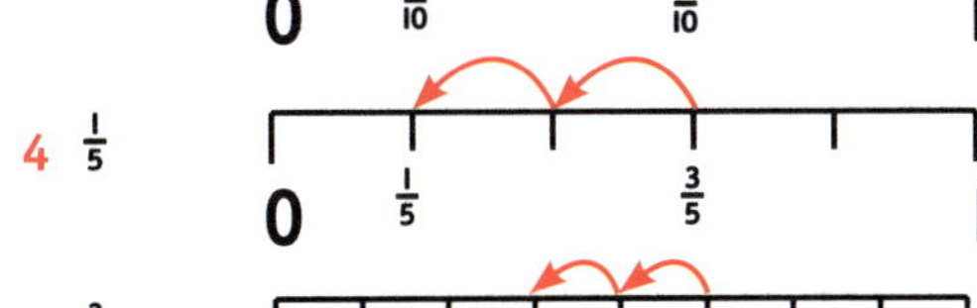

4 $\frac{1}{5}$

5 $\frac{3}{8}$

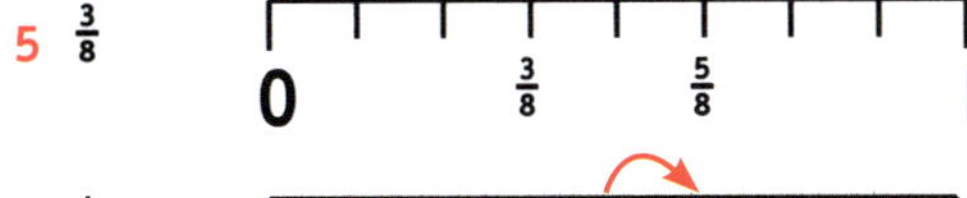

6 $\frac{1}{8}$

7 $\frac{1}{4}$

0 $\frac{1}{2}$ $\frac{3}{4}$ 1

8 $\frac{3}{8}$

0 $\frac{1}{8}$ $\frac{1}{2}$ 1

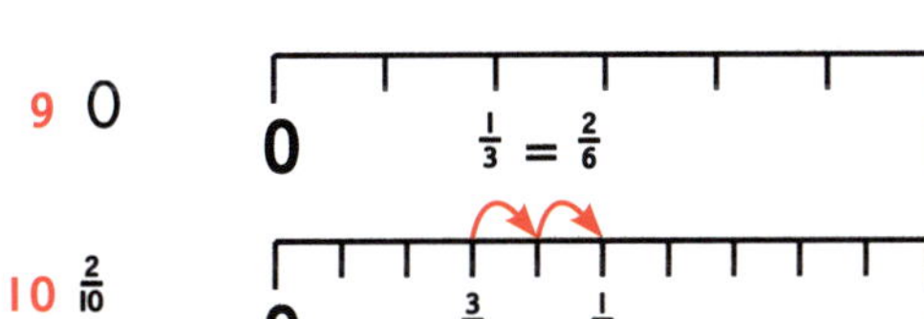

9 0

10 $\frac{2}{10}$

Unit 8

1 Step 1 $\frac{1}{5} \times 20 = 4$ Step 2 $3 \times 4 = 12$

Step 3 $\frac{3}{5} \times 20 = 12$

2 Step 1 $\frac{1}{8} \times 24 = 3$ Step 2 $3 \times 3 = 9$

Step 3 $\frac{3}{8} \times 24 = 9$

3 Step 1 $\frac{1}{6} \times 12 = 2$ Step 2 $5 \times 2 = 10$

Step 3 $\frac{5}{6} \times 12 = 10$

4 Step 1 $\frac{1}{5} \times 15 = 3$ Step 2 $2 \times 3 = 6$

Step 3 $\frac{2}{5} \times 15 = 6$

5 3 6 8 7 15 8 12

Unit 9

1 2

3 4

5 1250mL

6 $\frac{3}{4}$L

7 750mL

8 $1\frac{1}{4}$L

Unit 10

1 $\frac{1}{5} \times 20 = 4$

2 $\frac{9}{16}$

3 0.5 0·58 0·68 0.7

4 6

5 9 black, 18 white and 9 rust

6 10 minutes

7 Three $\frac{1}{2}$-litre jugs and one $\frac{1}{4}$-litre jug

8 Jake with $1\frac{7}{8}$

9 6:00pm, 8:00pm

10 100mL

Unit 11

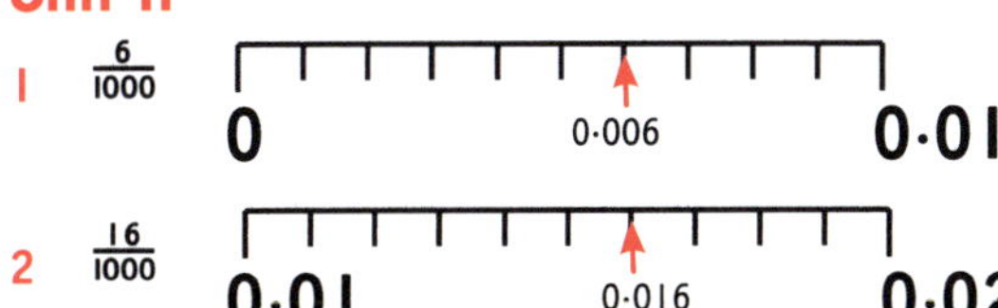

1 $\frac{6}{1000}$

2 $\frac{16}{1000}$

ANSWERS

3 $\frac{35}{1000}$ 0·03 — 0·035 — 0·04

4 $\frac{346}{1000}$ 0·34 — 0·346 — 0·35

5 0·007, $\frac{7}{1000}$

6 0·015, $\frac{15}{1000}$

7 0·043, $\frac{43}{1000}$

8 0·146, $\frac{146}{1000}$

Unit 12

1 1·8, 2
2 3·6, 4
3 3·5, 4
4 6·7, 7
5 8·6, 9
6 2·89, 2·9, 3
7 3·44, 3·4, 3
8 4·38, 4·4, 4
9 3·46, 3·5, 4
10 3·52, 3·5, 4

Unit 13

1 rounds up to 37, rounds up to 25, less than, 62
2 rounds down to 43, rounds down to 47, more than, 90
3 rounds up to 33, rounds down to 17, less than, 16
4 rounds up to 35, rounds down to 17, less than, 18
5 rounds up to 14, rounds up to 27, less than, 41
6 rounds down to 27, rounds up to 37, more than, 64
7 rounds down to 36, rounds up to 20, more than, 16
8 rounds up to 100, rounds up to 50, less than, 50

Unit 14

1 0·875
2 0·8
3 0·625
4 0·67
5 0·78
6 2·5
7 7
8 5·17
9 4·125
10 3·57

Unit 15

1 Step 1 3 × 3 = 9
Step 2 3 × 0·01 = 0·03
Step 3 9 − 0·03 = 8·97

2 Step 1 5 × 4 = 20
Step 2 5 × 0·25 = 1·25
Step 3 20 − 1·25 = 18·75

3 Step 1 3 × 4 = 12
Step 2 3 × 0·09 = 0.27
Step 3 12 + 0·27 = 12·27

4 Step 1 4 × 4 = 16
Step 2 4 × 0·5 = 2
Step 3 4 × 0·05 = 0·2
Step 4 16 + 2 + 0·2 = 18·2

5 Step 1 3 × 3 = 9
Step 2 3 × 0·3 = 0·9
Step 3 3 × 0·06 = 0·18
Step 4 9 + 0·9 + 0·18 = 10·08

6 Step 1 3 × 5 = 15
Step 2 3 × 0·1 = 0·3
Step 3 3 × 0·07 = 0·21
Step 4 15 + 0·3 + 0·21 = 15·51

Unit 16

1 4·9 × 10 = 49
2 3·67 × 100 = 367
3 4·08 × 100 = 408
4 5·679 × 1000 = 5679
5 36 ÷ 100 = 0·36
6 15 ÷ 100 = 0·15
7 325 ÷ 1000 = 0·325
8 4563 ÷ 10000 = 0·4563

Unit 17

1 $\frac{6}{3} = 2$

2 $\frac{6}{5} = 1\frac{1}{5}$

3 $\frac{9}{4} = 2\frac{1}{4}$

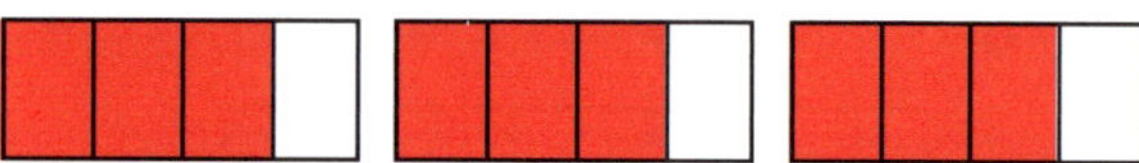

4 $\frac{1}{2} \times \frac{8}{1} = \frac{8}{2} = 4$

5 $\frac{4}{5} \times \frac{4}{1} = \frac{16}{5} = 3\frac{1}{5}$

6 $\frac{2}{3} \times \frac{6}{1} = \frac{12}{3} = 4$

7 $\frac{1}{4} \times \frac{4}{1} = \frac{4}{4} = 1$

8 $\frac{7}{8} \times \frac{3}{1} = \frac{21}{8} = 2\frac{5}{8}$

Unit 18

1 Step 1 36 × 10 = 360 and 0·9 × 10 = 9
Step 2 360 ÷ 9 = 40

2 Step 1 35 × 10 = 350 and 0·7 × 10 = 7
Step 2 350 ÷ 7 = 50

3 Step 1 36 × 10 = 360 and 0·4 × 10 = 4
Step 2 360 ÷ 4 = 90

4 Step 1 63 × 10 = 630 and 0·7 × 10 = 7
Step 2 630 ÷ 7 = 90

5 Step 1 56 × 100 = 5600 and 0·07 × 100 = 7
Step 2 5600 ÷ 7 = 800

6 Step 1 81 × 100 = 8100 and 0·09 × 100 = 9
Step 2 8100 ÷ 9 = 900

Unit 19

1 Step 1 0·8 × 10 = 8
Step 2 32 × 8 = 256
Step 3 256 ÷ 10 = 25·6

2 Step 1 0·5 × 10 = 5
Step 2 36 × 5 = 180
Step 3 180 ÷ 10 = 18

ANSWERS

3 Step 1 $0.9 \times 10 = 9$
Step 2 $27 \times 9 = 243$
Step 3 $243 \div 10 = 24.3$
4 Step 1 $0.8 \times 10 = 8$
Step 2 $24 \times 8 = 192$
Step 3 $192 \div 10 = 19.2$
5 Step 1 $0.7 \times 10 = 7$
Step 2 $35 \times 7 = 245$
Step 3 $245 \div 10 = 24.5$
6 Step 1 $0.12 \times 100 = 12$
Step 2 $37 \times 12 = 444$
Step 3 $444 \div 100 = 4.44$
7 Step 1 $0.14 \times 100 = 14$
Step 2 $42 \times 14 = 588$
Step 3 $588 \div 100 = 5.88$

Unit 20

1 $\frac{1}{10} \times 135 = 13.5$

2 $\frac{1}{100} \times 135 = 1.35$

3 $\frac{1}{2} \times 168 = 84$

4 $\frac{1}{10} \times 75 = 7.5$

5 Step 1 10% of 200 = 20
Step 2 1% of 200 = 2
Step 3 20 + 2 = 22
6 Step 1 20% of 200 = 40
Step 2 1% of 200 = 2
Step 3 40 + 2 = 42
7 Step 1 10% of 200 = 20
Step 2 5% of 200 = 10
Step 3 20 + 10 = 30
8 Step 1 20% of 200 = 40
Step 2 2% of 200 = 4
Step 3 40 + 4 = 44

Test 1

1 0 $\frac{3}{8}$ 1

0 $\frac{2}{5}$ 1

2 $\frac{6}{12}$ or $\frac{1}{2}$

3 $\frac{5}{6} + \frac{1}{3} = 1\frac{1}{6}$

0 1 2

4 0.6 or $\frac{60}{100}$ or $\frac{6}{10}$

5

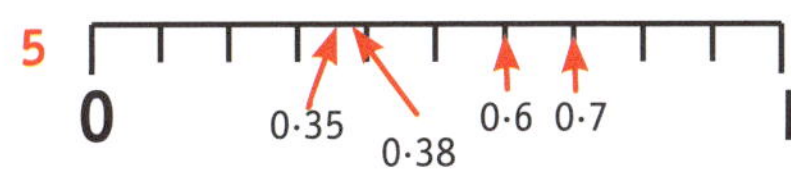

6

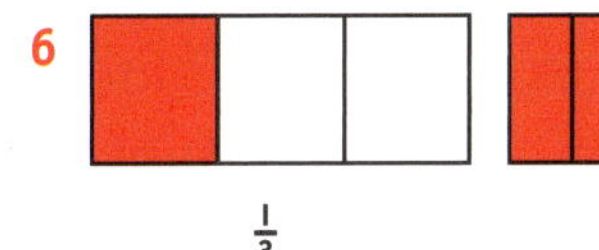

$\frac{1}{3}$

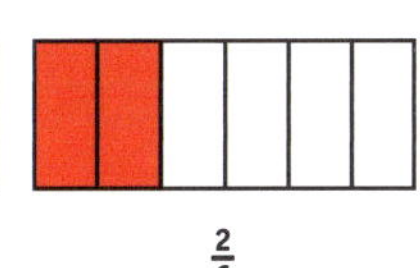

$\frac{2}{6}$

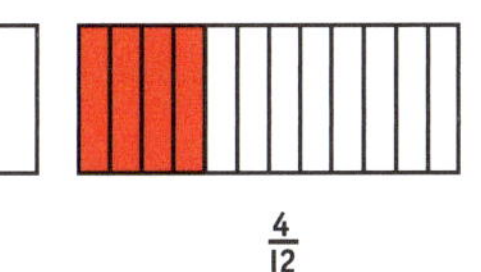

$\frac{4}{12}$

7 0 $\frac{3}{8}$ $\frac{3}{4}$ 1

8 Step 1 $\frac{1}{8} \times 32 = 4$
Step 2 $3 \times 4 = 12$
Step 3 $\frac{3}{8} \times 32 = 12$

9

10

Test 2

1

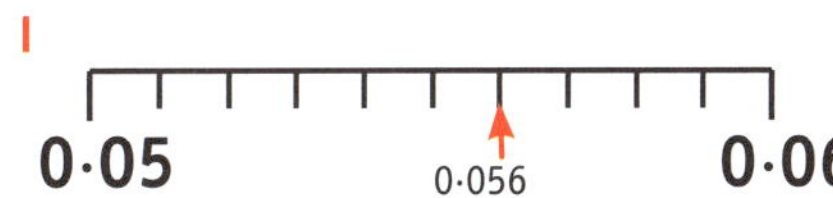

2 9.96 rounds to 10
8.876 rounds to 9
8.339 rounds to 8

3 13.786 rounds up to 14
36.576 rounds up to 37 less than 51
The answer will be close to, but less than, 51

4 0.625

5 Step 1 $5 \times 7 = 35$
Step 2 $35 - 0.55 = 34.45$

6 $0.36 \times 100 = 36$
$0.488 \times 1000 = 488$

7 $\frac{2}{3} \times \frac{12}{1} = \frac{24}{3} = 8$

8 Step 1 $0.3 \times 10 = 3$
Step 2 $33 \times 3 = 99$
Step 3 $99 \div 10 = 9.9$

9 Step 1 $54 \times 10 = 540$
Step 2 $0.9 \times 10 = 9$
Step 3 $540 \div 9 = 60$

10 25

Back to Basics Fractions & Decimals Years 5–6

Reprinted 2015, 2016, 2018

ISBN: 978 1 74215 933 1

Published by Pascal Press
PO Box 250
Glebe NSW 2037
www.pascalpress.com.au
contact@pascalpress.com.au

Author: Ann Baker
Publisher: Lynn Dickinson
Editor: Eliza Hope
Proofreader: Tim Learner
Design and illustration: Janice Bowles
Page layout and technical illustration: Louise Rhodes
Cover design: Deb Snibson, MAPG
Printed by Thumbprints